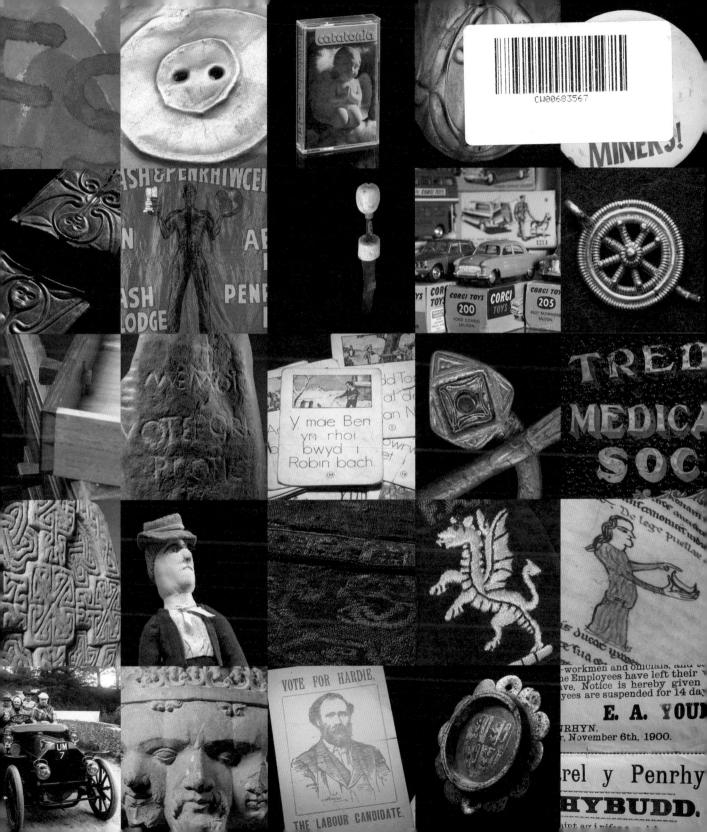

WALES IN 100 OBJECTS

First published in 2018 by Gomer Press,
Llandysul, Ceredigion SA44 4JL

Reprinted 2019

ISBN 978 1 78562 158 1
A CIP record for this title is available from the British Library.

This book is published with the financial support of the
Welsh Books Council.

Design: Rebecca Ingleby Davies

Printed and bound in Wales at
Gomer Press, Llandysul, Ceredigion
www.gomer.co.uk

Andrew Green has worked as a librarian and information director in universities
in Wales and England, and was Librarian of the National Library of Wales between 1998
and 2013. He has contributed to the work of many bodies, including the British Council,
the Welsh Government and the Coleg Cymraeg Cenedlaethol. He is President of the
Royal Institution of South Wales and chairs the Board of the *New Welsh Review*.
As 'gwallter', he publishes a weekly blog, and combines writing with long-distance walking.

Rolant Dafis is an independent photographer with over 20 years' experience working with
many and varied clients, encompassing the editorial, architectural and advertising
& marketing fields, as well as fine and contemporary art galleries and auction houses.
He began his career in Wales in the late 80s photographing the burgeoning
alternative Welsh-language music scene, and worked as a senior photographer for
Sotheby's in the early and mid-2000s. His eclectic list of clients also includes
The Independent, *The Guardian*, Christie's, and Creation Records.

WALES IN
100
OBJECTS

ANDREW GREEN

Photographs by Rolant Dafis

CONTENTS

INTRODUCTION

This book tells some of the stories of Wales, from the Neanderthals to now, using as its starting point one hundred objects that anyone can go and see.

Objects, even ones that look insignificant, can do powerful things. Sometimes they're intended to be powerful, to wield authority, like a sword or a king's sceptre. They can gain charisma over time, through extreme antiquity or the accident of rarity or through association with a critical event. Or they can remain ordinary but, for one reason or another, can be helped to tell a remarkable story.

Objects are not historical texts. While histories tend to reflect the standpoint of rulers and victors, objects can help redress the balance. They allow us to glimpse the lives of ordinary people, of women and children, and of the vanquished, whose voices often fail to reach the written record. There's another difference. Books usually aim to tell a single story, like the history of a country or the biography of a person. Objects, on the other hand, are open to being narrated through many, sometimes conflicting, histories. They can't speak themselves, but they can be interrogated from many different angles – returning us to the original meaning of the Greek word *historia*, an investigation.

It's rare for an object to tell a single story. More often, it will draw you in several directions, sometimes across lengthy periods of time. From a small toy and the box containing it (Object 91), threads can be followed not only to the lives of children, but also to refugees fleeing Nazi Germany, the experience of women working in factories, and the development of the Welsh car industry. Objects don't belong only to the time when they were made – they can have a long afterlife. Their original function can be forgotten, or seriously misinterpreted. They might acquire a new symbolic significance they were never intended to have.

All the objects in this book are public objects. But while many of them were intended to have a public use or impact, others started life as private things and many of them bore very personal associations. They were, to use Sherry Turkle's phrase, 'companions to the emotional lives' of individual people in the past. Today all of them still have the potential to touch us and provoke our thought, by demolishing, for a moment at least, the distance between their time and ours.

Teachers and curators have long known that one of the best ways to excite an interest in history and its ideas is to begin with a real thing: 'no ideas but in things',

The first Corgi toy made by the Mettoy Company Ltd, Fforestfach, Swansea, 1956

CORGI TOYS

200

FORD CONSUL
SALOON

CORGI
TOYS

200

FORD CONSUL SALOON

INTRODUCTION

as the poet William Carlos Williams wrote. The best place to see these real things is a memory institution. Each object illustrated in this book can be found in a museum, archive, library or other place open to the public in Wales. There's no substitute for encountering original objects at first hand, in the place where they're kept, but we hope that this book is a satisfying substitute or pointer. Rolant Dafis's images present the objects in vivid photographic detail. Beside each illustration is a text giving a few insights into their background, associations and history, and information about where they can be seen in the flesh.

Choosing the objects has been far from easy, and restricting their number to a hundred has been harder still. In part the choice has been guided by the need to strike several kinds of balance – of period, of place and of subject. Most periods of history and prehistory are represented, but with a weighting towards objects dating after around 1800. This bias reflects not only the increasing complexity of Welsh society from the early nineteenth century, but also the age profile of collection items in Welsh museums, archives and libraries. Care has been taken to select objects made or discovered across all geographical areas of Wales. Similarly, while about a third of the objects come from the collections of Amgueddfa Cymru – National Museum Wales and the National Library of Wales, the rest are from local institutions in every corner of the country *(see p 209 for a complete list)*. The range of themes is as broad as it can be, designed to illuminate many aspects of the political, economic, social and cultural life of Wales. Subjects include warfare and social rebellion, religion and belief, roads and railways, music and education, sport and popular culture. A further kind of balance is that of media. As well as three-dimensional objects, including tools and weapons, stones and sculptures, coins and notes, machines and toys, there are drawings, paintings and photographs, archival and printed documents, and maps and plans.

There are a few restrictions. All the objects are 'made objects': natural things unworked by human hand have been excluded. Buildings are too large and complex to count as 'objects'. No explicit attempt has been made to treat the Welsh outside Wales, though interactions between Wales and the world form a constant incidental theme. Only objects that anyone can visit and look at, usually in a collection open to the public, have been admitted.

This is not intended to be a treasury of the best or best-known objects of Wales. Some of them may be familiar or beautiful, but many are not. But all have been chosen for their intrinsic interest and for the richness of their associations. Some of the stories or people mentioned in them recur more than once throughout the book. Objects seem to speak to one another across time and space. Some of these connections are signalled in the text by cross-references from one object number to another. These draw attention to a surprising number of themes that recur, often many times, across centuries – for example, the Druids, resistance to injustice, and the links between Wales and slavery.

I'm grateful to many people for suggesting objects for inclusion. In the end, however, the final choice is a personal one. Though I've tried to accommodate the champions of some objects, I've not always heeded their advice. Inevitably, therefore, the selection reflects my own interests, enthusiasms and prejudices.

I'm happy to defend my choices and what I say about them. But that would be beside the point. Each person will have his or her own personal selection of a hundred objects, and each object will stimulate very different reactions. This book will have served one of its purposes if it excites readers to think about the objects they consider best represent Wales and its histories.

A second aim is to encourage readers to visit the archives, museums and libraries of Wales. Our country has a large number of memory institutions – not only the large national bodies like the National Library of Wales, but hundreds of local ones, scattered across all counties. Their combined collections include millions of objects, available for everyone to see, directly or on request. Most of the institutions are dependent on public funding. Their services and staffing have suffered during the long years of austerity imposed by UK governments and from a weakened commitment to the public realm. But through ingenuity and determination they continue to give a home and a stage to the material remains of Wales's past. Their collections are far from static. New discoveries of ancient objects are made every month, for example by metal detectorists. Objects from our own times continuously enter collections. And objects already in collections can reveal new information, thanks to scientific analysis and conservation work.

Today we can all pursue objects and their complex histories for ourselves. We can gather information from judicious use of the internet and its search engines. We can browse and search sources like the texts of newspapers and periodicals in ways impossible only twenty years ago. Online information, though, hasn't removed the need to explore printed and archival resources. Libraries and archives, still fertile ground for the object hunter, offer us their own pleasures of discovering new knowledge.

I hope you'll sense some of my enjoyment in the process of investigating the objects in this book, and that you'll be inspired to subject your own chosen objects to a similar interrogation.

Andrew Green
July 2018

1 Pontnewydd Cave handaxe
c.230,000 BCE

In the beginning, ice was critical. It was ice that determined whether or not the country we now call Wales could support human life. When glaciers engulfed the land and temperatures rarely rose above freezing point, life was impossible. More rarely, when the ice receded, the climate grew warmer, plants and animals flourished, and hominins – early forms of our own human species – were able to survive and reproduce.

About 230,000 years ago, during one such warmer period, a cave in Denbighshire sheltered the oldest humans known to have lived in Wales. Archaeologists working in Pontnewydd Cave, in the Elwy valley near St Asaph, between 1978 and 1995 revealed human teeth belonging to at least five individuals, children as well as adults. The teeth could be dated through a study of the sediments in which they were found. Laboratory analysis showed that they shared features such as an enlarged pulp chamber and short roots (taurodontism) typical of an early form of Neanderthal.

Neanderthals, named after a site in Germany where they were first identified, were descended from an ancestor they shared with our own species, *Homo sapiens sapiens*. Compared with us, they were short but very well-built, which made them well-adapted to cold weather. Their foreheads were ridged under the eyebrows, and they had large, wide noses and square, projecting jaws, as well as larger teeth. They had arrived in Wales overland from Europe – what is now the English Channel was not water at this time – and Pontnewydd Cave is their most north-westerly location recorded so far in Europe. Here they found they could make a living from hunting and scavenging in low-lying steppes where wildlife was plentiful.

Pontnewydd Cave was probably a temporary shelter rather than a permanent home. It gives many clues about how its inhabitants lived. The teeth were found with tools their owners used to hunt and prepare for eating the animals they caught: spear-points, knives, handaxes and scrapers. These were expertly made to suit their different purposes. The handaxe opposite was made by chipping a lump of local volcanic rock. It was used for butchering meat, while the scrapers were for removing skin, for diet and clothing. Animals the Neanderthals caught and ate included bear, horse and bison (bones of a bear and a horse, each showing marks of butchery, have also been found in the cave), though they also probably ate vegetables. Whether or not the Neanderthal skeletons were buried in Pontnewydd Cave is not known; water from later glaciers washed through the cave, erasing the evidence for their campsites.

Neanderthals occupied parts of Wales at various times over thousands of years. A small group used Coygan Cave, near Laugharne in Carmarthenshire, around 50,000 years ago. No human bones were found there, but two triangular handaxes made from local stone were recovered from near the cave wall. Later, hyenas rather than humans occupied the cave. But, for reasons not clearly understood, Neanderthals died out as a species by around 30,000 years ago. During their final period they overlapped with modern humans, who may have played a part in their demise, but there are other theories, including failure to adapt to rapid climatic change. Recent DNA studies have suggested interbreeding between the two species. Whatever the explanation, the ice-sheets returned and the land was empty again.

2 Paviland Cave flints
c.32,000 BCE

Getting to Paviland Cave today is not easy. It calls for good timing to catch a low tide, and strong muscles to clamber over rocks, through water and up to a narrow opening in the limestone face. But 30,000 years ago the cliffs of south Gower overlooked not the Bristol Channel, but a wide plain, teeming with hyenas, wolves, bison, woolly rhinoceros, reindeer and brown bears. These animals left traces of their bones in the cave. But it was human bones that made the word Paviland famous through Europe.

In 1822, two local residents, Rev. John Evans and Daniel Davies, discovered animal bones and a mammoth tusk in the cave. William Buckland, the first Reader in Geology at the University of Oxford, was alerted to the discoveries, and in January 1823 he arrived to oversee the excavation. His team uncovered a human skeleton, laid out and 'enveloped by a coating of a kind of ruddle', a red dye staining the bones and the earth nearby. Buckland thought that the skeleton could not be of great age. At first he suggested that it belonged to a customs officer murdered by smugglers, then to a Roman female prostitute or witch. He had it removed to Oxford, and it gained the nickname of the Red Lady – though the skeleton turned out to be male.

Dating the bones is difficult, but the most recent isotope analysis suggests that the Red Lady lived around 32,000 years ago, in the early Upper Palaeolithic Age – the oldest modern human found in Wales, and one of the oldest in Britain. (It was around this time that Neanderthals [1] disappeared from the archaeological record.) He was a young man, laid out in a ceremonial burial along the cave wall, with limestone slabs at head and foot. Personal ornaments – bones,

antlers, ivory rods and perforated seashell necklaces – had been placed with the body, which was covered with red ochre, probably taken from a source of iron oxide in the plain below. He was an individual of unusual importance in his community.

Paviland Cave was probably not used as a permanent home but as a place of ritual or as a safe store for possessions. It had a long history of use. Several excavations have uncovered not just bones and teeth, but over 4,000 flints and worked objects, made over thousands of years. Odo Vivian, later Baron Swansea, found the flints illustrated opposite in a cave hunting excavation in 1909. A Mousterian flake and some blade leaf-points hint at a Neanderthal presence in the cave. But the main uses of the cave by modern humans were during the Upper Palaeolithic period. Some of the earliest – Aurignacian blades, burins and scrapers – were made before the arrival of the Red Lady. Other flints date to the same period as him, others again to the time after the last ice advance in the Late Upper Palaeolithic and after. Many of the flints are thought to have been imported into the area.

Analysis of the Red Lady's bones shows that his diet consisted in part of fish. The nearest large river lay many miles away, and the sea even further, so it may be that people of the time were nomads living at some distance from the Gower cliffs, and that they used Paviland Cave for occasional and special purposes.

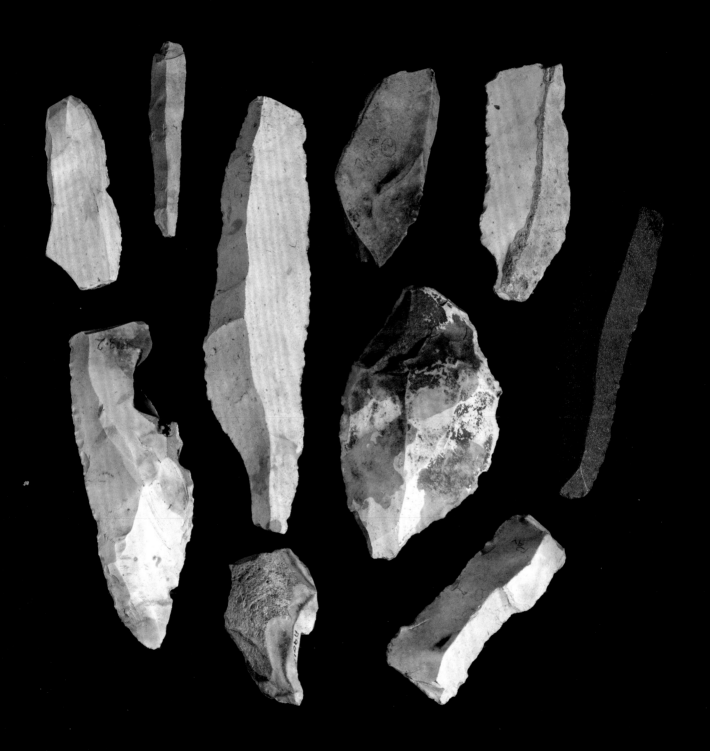

3 Maesmor macehead

c.3000 BCE

It is tempting to believe that, before the coming of worked metal, people in Wales scratched a simple, subsistence living with the help of a few primitive stone tools. The Neolithic macehead from Maesmor suggests this view is exaggerated.

A workman clearing ground in a wood on the Maesmor estate near Y Rug, Denbighshire came across the object in 1840. It is a small tool, 76mm long, made of creamy flint, a stone very rare in the area. Its maker carefully drilled a neat round hole through the stone, off-centre, to house a wooden haft or handle. Then the artist smoothed the hard stone to a regular shape, and with the help of a bow-drill began to weave a complex pattern all round it – leaving just one small blemish where the last surface fails to meet the first. To produce an object of this intricacy and finish would have required a very practised eye and hand, and many hours of concentrated work.

Maces may have originated in clubs used in warfare, but other roughly contemporary examples found in Wales and beyond show few signs of heavy use. It seems to have been used as a public symbol of power or prestige, and may have been displayed in ceremonies as a proof of the high status of its owner, perhaps a chieftain or other dignitary. On stylistic grounds the mace can be dated to around 3000 BCE, in the middle of the Neolithic period.

The Neolithic inhabitants of Wales may have been farmers as well as hunters, and their economy, if it was based in part on crops and domesticated animals,

was well developed. They could tame parts of their environment, clearing woodland for cultivation and grazing. They could produce surpluses and trade more widely than earlier peoples. Their communities were more settled, populations increased and society became more complex. New technologies, like pottery-making for storing and cooking food, emerged.

The most obvious signs today of the complexity of Neolithic societies in Wales are the hundred or so megalithic graves scattered across the country. The large structures at Parc le Breos in Gower, Tinkinswood in the Vale of Glamorgan and Pentre Ifan in Pembrokeshire could only have been built by well-organised communities united in a common purpose. How their societies were structured is hidden from us, but we know something of their economy. They produced and distributed stone implements, especially axe heads, on a large scale. At Graig Lwyd above Penmaenmawr are the remains of an 'axe factory', where tools were split from the native igneous rock. Off-site, they were shaped, smoothed and exported: tools from the site have been found in all parts of Britain and in Ireland. Graig Lwyd can fairly be called one of the first centres of industry in Wales.

The mace is still used today in Wales as a symbol of authority. When the 2006 session of the National Assembly for Wales began, a new mace was placed in the Chamber, a gift of the government of New South Wales, Australia.

Mace in the Senedd Chamber (National Assembly for Wales)

4. Gold sun-disc
2500-2000 BCE

It was the Danish archaeologist Christian Thomsen who, in the 1820s, first divided prehistory into successive ages of stone, bronze and iron. His idea, grounded in the reality of objects found in the earth, might overemphasise what we would now call technological determinism. But it has lasted well. Certainly the discovery and spread of bronze working did mark big changes in human society and economy. Metal tools allowed people to work wood and other materials, and so improve their daily lives. They also made more efficient weapons for communities to attack other groups and extend their power. The population may have grown considerably.

As well as smelting and working copper and tin to make bronze, technologists could also work skilfully with other metals, like gold. The Copa Hill gold disc was discovered in 2002 by an archaeologist exploring a Roman and medieval lead hearth near Cwmystwyth, Aberystwyth (an opencast Bronze Age copper mine lies just 200m away). The disc came from a burial found close by. It may have been attached like a large button (it is about 39mm in diameter), by its two perforated holes, to the funeral robe of the grave's occupant. It can be dated to between 2500 and 2000 BCE – the Copper Age, before the beginning of the Bronze Age – by comparison with other, similar sun-discs found elsewhere, especially in Ireland. Where the almost pure gold came from is not known. It may have come from elsewhere, although gold was also available in Wales, which has yielded many other gold objects, including torcs, bracelets, rings and the boat-shaped Caergwrle bowl.

It would be unsurprising if the disc came from outside Wales. Travel and trade, linked to the search for metal, extended over far greater distances than before, especially across the Irish Sea and along the Atlantic seaboard. Travel by water was far easier than by land and Bronze Age peoples were experienced sailors.

The symbolic significance of the disc is unclear. Its likeness to a sun may be no coincidence, and the circles, three lined, two dotted, made by a *repoussé* technique (punching decoration from behind the hammered and polished thin sheet) may also carry a lost meaning. What is clear is that its owner was a person of standing and substance. The fortunate few, like the wearer of the exotic ceremonial Mold Cape, now in the British Museum, were proud to exhibit their golden wealth.

We know much more about the dead than about the living population of Bronze Age Wales. Traces of their settlements are sparse, but the country is dotted with their burial sites, cairns and barrows, often clustered in groups and occupying upland locations. Built of stones or earth, these circular mounds usually contain the buried, and later cremated, remains of one or more than one person, together with their possessions.

Copa Hill and other copper mining sites, like the underground workings at the Great Orme near Llandudno, also give us an insight into how some people made a living. They used sophisticated techniques to extract the copper: fire and water to crack the rocks, hammerstones and antler picks to break them, and drains to remove water. There was no tin to be found in Wales, so transport was needed to unite Welsh copper with Cornish tin to make bronze alloy.

5 Llyn Cerrig Bach hoard
c.400 BCE–100 CE

Anglesey, the Roman historian Tacitus says, was a focus of British resistance to Roman military power. The island was populous, and said to be a shelter for refugees and the centre of power of the Druidae or Druids. As they prepared to invade in the year 60 CE, Roman soldiers could see, across the Menai Strait, 'ranks of armed men, and among them women dressed in black like Furies, with flying hair and flaring torches; and around them Druids, their hands raised to heaven, poured out dreadful curses'. The Romans crossed the Strait, killed those they caught, and destroyed the sacred groves where, it was said, the natives would sacrifice their prisoners and appease their gods.

The Druids later attracted many myths [49], but we know from other literary sources that they were a distinct social group, holding a position of honour in Celtic societies. Tacitus seems to have been right in thinking that Anglesey held a special place in the religious culture of the Iron Age inhabitants of Wales.

In 1943 William Owen Roberts was helping to prepare a new runway at RAF Valley. While lifting peat from the southern edge of Llyn Cerrig Bach, he came across an iron chain. At first he failed to realise its significance, and even used it to haul a lorry from the mud. Further excavations in the waterlogged peat brought to light a rich hoard of over 160 prehistoric iron, bronze and other objects. They had been placed in the lake, probably over a period of at least 100 years, as gifts for the water gods. Some of the objects had been deliberately broken.

The iron chain was designed to shackle five prisoners, or more likely slaves. Most ancient societies practised slavery, and we know from the writer Strabo that slaves were exported from Britain to the Roman empire before the conquest. The other objects include swords, spearheads, fragments of a shield, part of a bronze trumpet, fragments of at least ten different chariots or wagons, horse gear, blacksmith's tools, cauldrons and four iron bars used for trading. The most striking object is a moon-shaped bronze plaque, possibly fixed to a shield or chariot. Its decoration features a triskele, or symmetrical triple spiral. The triskele is a characteristically British variant of the La Tène style, named after a site in Switzerland but common across the Celtic world.

In recent years, researchers have questioned the use of the term 'Celts' when referring to the Iron Age inhabitants of Europe. The Celts may not have formed a single ethnic grouping, and few now believe that there was ever a Celtic or Iron Age invasion of Britain from the continent. But many parts of northern Europe undoubtedly shared a common artistic culture, with regional variations, as well as a common family of languages, from which the modern Celtic languages derive.

The variety and richness of the Llyn Cerrig Bach hoard suggest that the lake was a ceremonial site of more than local importance. Some of the objects came from Wales, but others came from southern England, Ireland or even further. Some show signs of Roman influence, and it is likely that the deposits were made over a long period, before and after the invasion. Together the objects reflect a well-organised society, technologically sophisticated, militarily well-equipped and connected with many other centres.

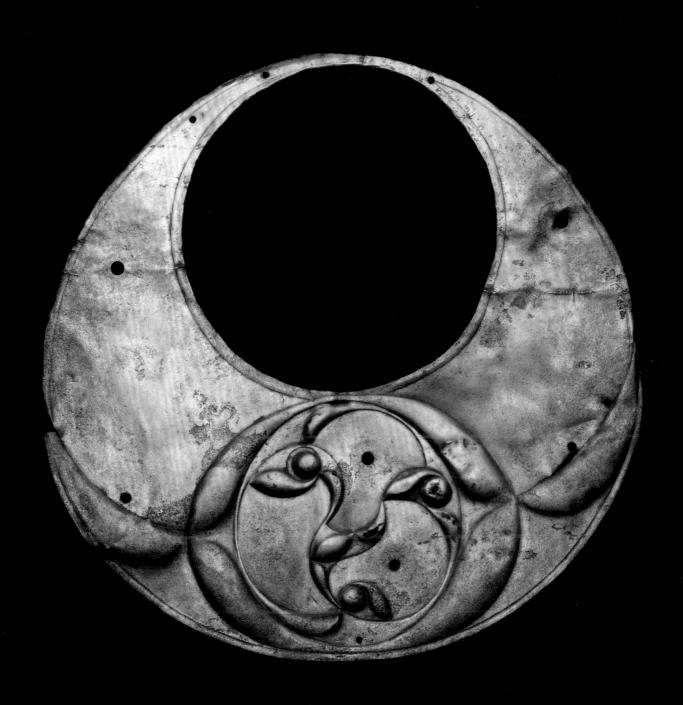

6 Capel Garmon firedog
1-100 CE

Before 1000 BCE Wales was becoming wetter and colder. This climatic change and other, human factors affected where people lived. They tended to migrate from upland to lowland areas. Enclosures, conventionally called hillforts, sprang up throughout the country as the typical kind of settlement. Over 1,000 of them survive. Though some were well-defended, many were not built on hills, and many were not primarily military in nature. They served as animal enclosures, grain stores or religious centres, as well as farms and small villages, characterised by round wooden houses. Though settlements were small and well scattered, by the time the Romans arrived in Britain political power had consolidated into larger groupings or tribes, whose leaders commanded large regions of Wales.

There was another change. By around 800 BCE iron was beginning to be used in Wales. Iron tools made it easier to work the land and later on iron weapons made warfare more lethal. Ore was smelted in clusters of furnaces in Merioneth and probably elsewhere. Skilled blacksmiths worked the metal into tools and weapons for local communities throughout Wales. One of them, a highly accomplished craftsman, was active at some time during the first century CE near Capel Garmon, Betws-y-coed.

In 1852 a farm worker digging peaty ground at Carreg Goedog near Capel Garmon found an iron object, about a metre in length. It had been deliberately buried, having been laid on its side and pinned at each end by two large stones. It turned out to be a highly ornate firedog – originally placed, probably with a twin, by the hearth at the centre of a round house.

Other firedogs of the same period have been found, mainly in south-east England, but the Capel Garmon one is unique in its flamboyant elaboration and technical virtuosity. Each of its uprights culminates in an animal motif, combining an ox's horned head with the neck and dressed mane of a horse. Artists who shared the La Tène style [5] common throughout the later Iron Age often represented animals in simplified and stylised form, but this is a particularly rococo example. In 1991 the Pembrokeshire sculptor and blacksmith David Petersen made two replicas of the Capel Garmon firedog, based on X-rays of the original. He used 85 separate iron pieces, including 30 rivets and 34 applied heads. Without doubt the firedog is the product of advanced craftwork and artistic imagination, and was an exceptionally valuable object. Producing it, from smelting to finished item, probably took three years' work.

The firedog's careful burial in a watery location suggests that it may have been offered as a votive gift to a river or lake god, perhaps on the death of its wealthy owner (unlike other firedogs, it seems not to have been part of a human cremation). There are several other examples in Wales, like the Llyn Cerrig Bach hoard [5], of prestigious objects being deposited in or near lakes.

Less than a mile from Capel Garmon lies a large chambered tomb. It was originally built in the Neolithic period, but pottery finds show that it was still in use in the early Bronze Age. The tomb and firedog are separated in time by 3,000 years, but it is not impossible that the ironsmith and the tomb users belonged to a community that had settled and then remained in the location.

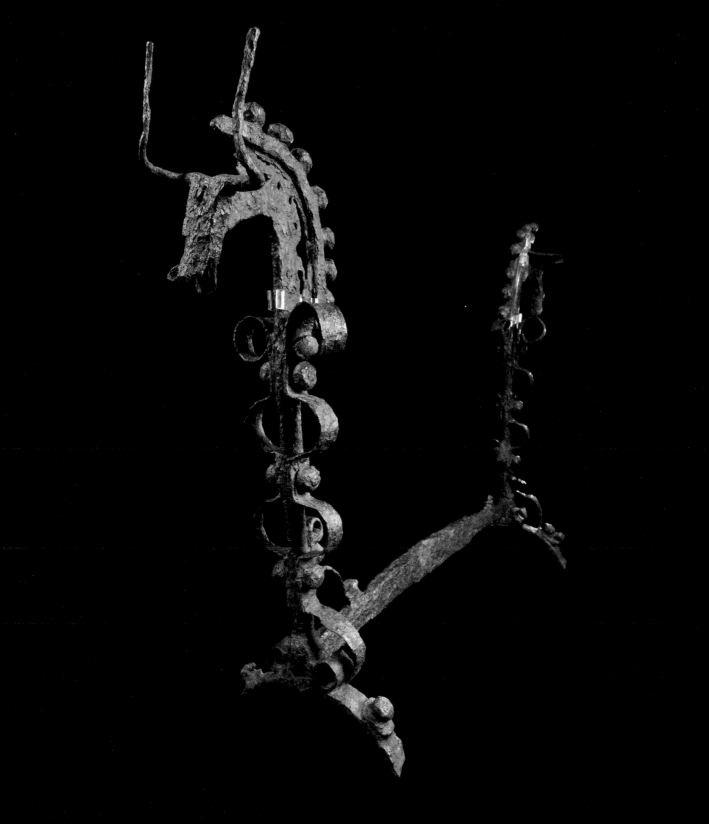

7 Langstone tankard
40-70 CE

Roman writers often noted with distaste that the peoples who lived beyond the northern borders of their empire were fond of communal drinking and feasting. The Gauls, they reported, drank imported wine, unmixed with water, and beer made from barley and wheat. They took draughts, little but often, from a common cup. Drunkenness was frequent.

Iron Age Britons too had a serious drinking culture. Archaeological evidence of drinking vessels is common, especially in southern and western Britain. Two tankards of outstanding quality come from Wales, one with concave sides and an elaborately decorated handle discovered near Trawsfynydd in the nineteenth century, the other found in 2007 by a metal detectorist, Craig Mills, in a field near Langstone, east of Newport.

The Langstone vessel, undisturbed for centuries in waterlogged soil, was exceptionally well-preserved. It was made of several elements. First, six vertical strips of yew wood were carved to a curved shape, carefully fitted together and slotted into a circular wooden base. Then an outer casing of two copper alloy sheets was added. These hoops were heated so that on cooling they fused together and fitted snugly onto the wooden core. Finally, a narrow copper strip was fixed to the lip of the tankard, and a single plain handle made of copper alloy was attached to the body by two plates and bronze rivets.

The tankard could have held about four pints of beer. It was not for individual use, but held in two hands and passed around a gathering of people, each person taking a draught before passing it on to the next. The occasion may have been formal or ceremonial, since the Langstone tankard is clearly not an everyday vessel. Feasts, of which drinking was a part, held social significance. They were occasions for reinforcing prestige, allegiance and wealth, and included secondary activities like gift-giving.

When the tankard was manufactured, and when it was deposited, is very difficult to say. It might have been made before or after the Roman invasion of Britain in 43 CE. About 13 metres away from where he found the tankard Craig Mills discovered a small hoard including two bronze bowls and a bronze wine strainer. These vessels were probably deposited at about the same period, but a firm dating for them is little easier. They may belong to the immediate pre-Roman period: their style is native – the strainer has a triskele pattern on its base [5] – and they seem to have been laid down near a lake or stream as a votive offering, according to Iron Age practice.

But if they are pre-Roman, a new age was about to begin. Langstone is just a few miles from Caerleon, the large fortress built in 74-5 CE to house the 2nd Augustan Legion as a base to conquer and pacify south Wales [12]. Roman military occupation soon led to civilian development, and only 350m from the Langstone site, at Ford Farm Villa, a Roman-style farm was built, probably before the end of the first century CE. It later developed into a regular villa, with two mosaic floors. The old order was changing – though probably not the old liking for drinking wine and beer. And influences moved in two directions: writing tablets from the fort of Vindolanda on Hadrian's Wall talk of local beer being enjoyed by Roman soldiers.

8 Tal-y-llyn relief
50-80 CE

One of the finest walks in Wales begins at Minffordd, north-east of Tal-y-llyn, climbs steeply through woods to Llyn Cau, and continues upwards to Craig Cau and Pen y Gadair, the summit of Cadair Idris. One summer day in 1963 two walkers took a diversion from the path to picnic near Nant Cadair, which streams through the woods. One of them noticed a bundle of metal objects lodged in a hole beneath a large glacial boulder. They were clearly of great antiquity.

Among the pieces the walkers found was a matching pair of carefully worked plaques, of trapezoid shape, probably attached to the fronts of wooden or leather shields. Made of brass (an alloy of copper and zinc) each thin sheet, 127mm in length, was decorated with stylised images of opposed human heads, attached to each other by a single long neck. The near-circular head features large staring eyes, an open mouth and finely engraved hair. Curved lines loop and swirl round the figures.

The theme and decoration of the plaques place them firmly in the La Tène art style [5, 6], common throughout northern Europe in the final centuries BCE. Sculpted stone heads are frequently found on Iron Age archaeological sites in France and Britain, often isolated within niches, and it is known from Roman sources that severed heads held social significance in warfare. But beyond that it is unsafe to go. Some writers have talked of a Celtic head cult, but with little evidence. It is just possible that the two heads of the Tal-y-llyn plaques represent a two-headed deity, whose role was to protect the shield's owner. Or that the severed heads were intended to protect the shields' owners from harm, or to terrify enemies and remind them of the grizzly fate in store for them should they be vanquished.

Other objects in the Tal-y-llyn collection included decorated shield bosses with triskele motifs [5], and plates from a cart or bier. Many of the objects are made of brass, an alloy rarely found before the Roman era, and there is what was been interpreted as a plate from a Roman lock. So it is likely that the cache was hidden after, or possibly just before, the Roman occupation of Wales, which began in the late 70s CE.

Researchers can only speculate about why the objects were left where they were found. Their owners may have hidden them for safety and later collection, at a time of danger – perhaps as the Roman legions advanced towards them. Or, more likely, they deposited the hoard as a gift, perhaps to a water god, since Nant Cadair is not far away, and an old spring arises nearby.

When and where the objects were made is even harder to determine. Most of them share similar stylistic features, and it could be that they were all manufactured in the same workshop, quite possibly in Wales or in the area in which they were found.

The location of the find suggests that the Minffordd route up the mountain was in use in prehistoric times. It would not be surprising if Iron Age people regularly climbed up the path to visit Llyn Cau, lying deep and dark in its cirque below the encircling crags of Cadair Idris and Mynydd Moel, to leave gifts for the gods who lived there.

9 Segontium sword
Late 1st – early 2nd century CE

Organised military violence was the Roman way with defiant enemies. After the initial invasion of Britain under the emperor Claudius in 43 CE Roman power expanded steadily across England. Highland Britain proved harder to subdue and costlier to garrison. In Wales the two largest peoples, the Silures and the Ordovices, fought back fiercely for over thirty years. After their conquest the Romans built two legionary fortresses, at Chester and Caerleon (at first, Usk), as well as a network of smaller forts and camps across Wales, linked by new roads.

They planted their main fort in the north-west at Segontium, above what is now Caernarfon. Agricola, governor of Britain (and father-in-law of the historian Tacitus) founded it in the late 70s CE, after he had defeated the Ordovices. From it the Romans could control the hinterland, the coasts and the fertile land of Anglesey, earlier a base of resistance [5]. The troops stationed there, up to a thousand strong, were infantry auxiliaries, made up of non-citizens from elsewhere in the Empire. In the early third century they were Sunici, a people from what is now the border between Belgium and Germany.

The sword was found in 1879 on a road in or near the perimeter of the fort. It is one of the most complete examples found in Britain of an iron *gladius*, the standard lightweight sword of a Roman soldier. At 50cm long it would have been lethal, with its sharp point and double-sided razor-edged blade. A soldier could use it either in close formation, or in individual combat to stab and to hack his opponent. The well-preserved handle consists of a guard, a grip made of wood and bone, and an egg-shaped pommel made of walrus ivory.

Outside the fort, to the west and south, a civilian settlement or *vicus* developed to serve the needs of the soldiers. At the beginning of the third century it contained a temple to Mithras, an eastern god often worshipped by Roman soldiers, and many of the inhabitants were probably retired soldiers and their families. In south Wales some settlements grew into larger, more formal towns like Caerwent [11] and Carmarthen, but in the north, where Roman influence was weaker, towns and villas failed to develop. Many native people continued to live in the settlements they had used before the Romans came, like the hillforts of Tre'r Ceiri in Llŷn and Din Silwy on Anglesey.

Segontium, unusually, kept a working garrison throughout the Roman period. Soldiers may have been needed in the fourth century to combat Irish coastal raiders, and the fort was still occupied in 394 CE. People probably continued to live in and around Segontium after military occupation ceased. The nearby church, just south of the Roman Mithraeum, is dedicated to St Peblig, a version of the Latin name Publicus.

Segontium also lived on in Welsh literary tradition. It occurs in *The dream of Macsen Wledig*, one of the Mabinogi stories, written perhaps early in the thirteenth century. Macsen – an echo of Magnus Maximus, the Roman commander of Britain proclaimed Emperor in 383 CE – dreams of a beautiful woman. The woman, called Elen, is tracked down at Aber Saint (the mouth of the Seiont), and there Macsen builds a fort for her. According to later tradition St Peblig was a son of Macsen and Elen.

10 Dolaucothi gold wheel pendant and chain

2nd or 3rd century CE

After their conquest of Wales, in the mid-70s CE the Romans built a new military fort at Pumsaint in the valley of the river Cothi in Carmarthenshire. It had a special purpose: to guard one of their most valuable industrial assets in Britain, the gold mines 800m away at Dolaucothi.

The Romans probably knew that gold had been mined here before they came. Before long they were using their advanced technological skills to extract it. They mined gold-bearing rocks at the surface or in adits, but they also sank stopes, or step-like excavations, to follow the gold-bearing lode underground. In one of them was found a fragment of a wooden wheel probably used to drain water from the workings. Water also played an important part in the industrial process – initially, to hush the ore, by removing earth and loose pebbles to expose the rock; in extraction, to ground-sluice or wash ore-bearing material down the slope; and in processing, to filter crushed ore and separate the dense gold. A large stone with rounded indentations, Carreg Pumsaint, may have been used by Roman engineers as a water-powered anvil in an ore-crushing stamp mill.

To collect water Roman engineers built leats. Their courses can still be traced today. One took its supply from the river Cothi, 11km up the valley, a second tapped the Nant Dar, a tributary of the Cothi, while a third may have originated from the river Gwenlais. Water stored in reservoirs was then released down gullies for use in the mine. Sextus Julius Frontinus, the governor of Britain probably responsible for building the Pumsaint fort, was later appointed as commissioner for the aqueducts of Rome and wrote a surviving report about them.

The gold mine would have been under direct military control, and the miners were no doubt slaves or convicts. Much of the gold may have been exported to the imperial mint in Lyon to produce coins. Some may have been worked by goldsmiths close to the site and used for very different purposes. At the end of the eighteenth and the beginning of the nineteenth century several personal ornaments made of gold were found at Dolaucothi. Among them was a chain, and a clasp or pendant in the form of a wheel with eight spokes (the British Museum houses pendants and bracelets from the same find). Similar Roman pendants have been found elsewhere in northern Europe. It is possible that the device refers to the Celtic thunder god Taranis, whose symbol was the chariot wheel (Taranis was conflated with the Roman god Jupiter).

The military fort, beneath the current village of Pumsaint, enclosed less than two hectares, and housed auxiliary soldiers. Around 120 CE it was reduced in size to less than a hectare, with a new stone wall, before being abandoned a few years later. Extramural settlements grew up to the east and south of the fort, and south of the river Cothi, nearer the gold mines, where a small bath-house, heated by a hypocaust system, came to light in 1831. This southern settlement briefly continued after the fort was abandoned. Perhaps military protection was no longer thought necessary; in any case, troops were needed to garrison northern England. The gold mines probably continued to be worked, perhaps even into the third century. Attempts were made to reopen the mines in the nineteenth century.

11 Two Caerwent gods
Roman period

'**They make a desert and call it peace,**' **said Calagacus,** a north British leader, about Roman imperial methods, according to the historian Tacitus. But the Romans had other ways of pacifying conquered peoples. One was to foster the growth of towns, as centres of local self-government and to help cultural and religious integration. At Caerwent, in the territory of the Silures, fierce resistors of Roman invasion, the town of Venta Silurum was developed. It may have grown out of a settlement flanking the main route between Gloucester and Caerleon towards the end of the first century, and was probably occupied at first by army veterans and traders. Eventually the town grew to cover around 18 hectares. A planned street grid of some 20 *insulae* or blocks included a market place and town hall, baths, shops and houses, some with mosaic floors. In the third century the town was surrounded by a substantial stone wall, large parts of which survive today. A stone inscription of around 220 CE records the existence of a self-governing *ordo*, or town council. The people of Venta Silurum would have become Roman citizens once the franchise was extended to all free men and women of the empire in 212 CE [12].

Religions from elsewhere in the Roman empire reached Caerwent, including Christianity by the fourth century. But older, British gods survived. Some were assimilated with Roman deities: a Romano-Celtic temple was found, and two inscriptions elsewhere mention a god who combined Roman Mars with native Ocelus. Two stone statuettes excavated in the town may depict pre-Roman gods, unaffected by Roman religions.

The first statuette, a head about 23cm high and made from local quartz sandstone, was found near a small building outside the back of a large fourth-century house. It was set on the remains of an altar approached by three shallow steps. Its simplified, mask-like forms – bulging eyes, geometric mouth, nose and recessed earholes – place the head within a common Celtic artistic tradition. The sculptor carved the back and base flat, so that it could fit into a niche or on a pedestal against a wall. There is no sign that the head belonged to a body. The continental Celts thought the human head was the seat of the soul. Some have thought that the Caerwent sculpture is a severed head translated into stone [8]. But more likely it was an image of a local god, still venerated centuries after the coming of Roman rule.

The second sculpture shares a similar style with the head and may have come from the same local workshop. About 27cm high, it shows a mother goddess, of a type well known in Celtic art. She sits, naked except for a hood on her head, on what looks like a high-backed armchair. She holds a round fruit in her left hand and a branch, possibly a fir tree, in her right. The statue was placed at the bottom of a deep pit near the temple site. She may embody the power of fertility. Or she may have possessed healing powers, like other Celtic goddesses whose names are known, like Coventina, Arnemetia and Sulis, who lent her name to Aquae Sulis, Roman Bath.

For 300 years Caerwent stood almost alone in Wales as a major urban centre, inhabited by people of many nationalities and religions.

12 Roman memorial from Caerleon
Probably 3rd century CE

Sometime in the early third century CE a woman called Tadia Exuperata decided to commemorate her dead mother and brother. Near Pil-bach, in a cemetery on what is now Lodge Hill, less than a mile from the legionary fortress of Caerleon, she paid for a Latin inscription to be cut, in clear capital letters, on a gabled stone:

> To the spirits of the departed. Tadia Vallaunius lived 65 years, and Tadius Exuper[a]tus, her son, lived 37 years, having died on the German expedition. Tadia Exuperata, the devoted daughter, set this up to her mother and brother beside her father's tomb.

Tadia Exuperata's father was very likely a soldier in the Second Augustan Legion, stationed at Caerleon. Perhaps he was an officer in the legion, which consisted, in theory at least, of about 5,500 soldiers and 120 troopers. They lived in barracks within the fortress but some had relationships, and children, with women living in the civil settlements or *canabae* that grew up outside.

The soldier's partner, Tadia Vallaunius, was possibly a local girl – the name Vallaunius is Celtic. Their son's name, Exuperatus, may also be Celtic. Tadius possibly followed his father into a military life. If the 'German expedition' Tadia mentions is the military one launched by the emperor Caracalla against the Alemanni, a people who lived in the upper Rhine valley, then he may have died in 212-3 CE.

The year 212 was a significant one for the whole Roman world. It was when the emperor Caracalla extended Roman citizenship, beyond Italians, legionary veterans, local town officials and other groups, to all free-born inhabitants of the empire. Why he made this decision, the biggest single grant of citizenship in history, is not certain, but its effect was to give about 30 million people a personal stake in Rome's constitution and laws.

Caracalla's father, Septimius Severus, had earlier enacted reforms that improved the conditions of serving soldiers. In around 197 CE he granted them the right to contract a legal marriage, giving their wives and offspring the right to inherit their money and property (legionaries were given a pension when they retired after 25 years of service). This change would have come too late for Tadia's father, but 'unofficial' family life was widely tolerated. This family was not lacking in wealth: inscriptions in stone were beyond the means of many of those living in Caerleon's extramural settlements, and Tadia's memorial, with its relief decorations of rosettes and a crescent moon, is one of only a handful to have survived intact from Caerleon. Most of the cremation burials excavated so far seem to have been unmarked, at least by stone.

A military career was secure and had its benefits, but life was dangerous. Julius Valens, a soldier mentioned in another Caerleon inscription, seems to have lived to be 100 years, but others, like Tadius, died young. Aurelius Herculanus, a trooper, died at 28, and Titus Flavius Candidus, an infantryman, at 27.

Parts of the fortress were probably being rebuilt at the time when Tadia and her family lived at Caerleon. An inscription records that Severus and his sons restored a building, perhaps the headquarters building, 'that had decayed through old age'. But by the early fourth century there was little or no military presence left and civilians may have taken over parts of the fortress.

D · M

TADAVALLAVNVS VIXIT
ANN · IXVETADVSEXVPERTVS
FLVSVIXTANXXXVIIDEFVN
TVSEXEDTONEGERMNCA
TADAEXVPERATAFLA
MATRETRATR · PIISSM A
SECVSTVMVLVM
PATRIS   POSVIT

13 Rogiet coin hoard
295-6 CE

People in Wales had little or no use for coins before the Romans came. After the invasion payment for soldiers and trade between the army and its suppliers meant that Roman coins became common in military areas. Their use gradually spread to fort settlements and towns, though more remote native communities rarely needed them.

In 1998 a metal detectorist working at Rogiet, around three kilometres south-west of the Roman town of Caerwent in Monmouthshire [11], found a hoard of 3,813 coins from the third century CE.

Hoards are not uncommon. Over 200 are known from Roman Wales, which has yielded in total over 66,000 coins. In times of uncertainty and danger there was good reason to conceal wealth suddenly. The Rogiet hoard, of mainly copper-alloy coins, was probably buried about 295-6 CE, when political crisis gripped Britain and the empire. Its coins span a period of 40 years. The series of over 20 emperors ends with coins issued by the usurper emperors Carausius (reigned 287-93) and Allectus (293-6) – with over 750 by the latter.

Carausius, born of humble stock in what is now Belgium, was commander of the British fleet, responsible for policing the seas. He was suspected of allowing pirates free rein in exchange for money he pocketed, and the western emperor Maximian ordered his death. Carausius, believing that attack was the best form of defence, declared himself emperor of Britain and northern Gaul. Backed by his fleet and legions from Britain and northern France, he managed to withstand attack. For some years he effectively shared power with the other two emperors before he was checked by Maximian and then assassinated by his lieutenant,

Allectus. Allectus in turn was defeated and killed in 296. So ended the first independent British state. The island returned to rule from Rome.

Coins were often used for promotion and propaganda as well as for financial exchange. Those of Carausius, many struck at his London mint, are no exception. One of them asserts his equal and collegial status with the other two emperors, Diocletian and Maximian. It shows the heads of the three in overlapping profile, and adds the words 'Carausius and his brothers'. On the reverse is 'Victoria Auggg' – the three 'g's another reference to the three joint 'Augusti'. Other coins, not represented in the Rogiet hoard, play on what seem to be feelings of British independence. One has the wording '*Restitutor Britanniae*' ('Restorer of Britain'), another '*Genio Britanni*' ('To the Spirit of Britain'). On a third is the abbreviation ('RSR') of a quotation from the poet Virgil beginning '*Redeunt Saturnia regna*' ('the Golden Age Returns'). Virgil is again the source for a rare silver issue, '*Expectate veni*' (come, Expected One') under an image of Britannia welcoming Carausius. These messages imply he was able to appeal to supporters in Britain who were both highly literate and proud of their island identity.

No doubt Carausius and Allectus came and went without disturbing the lives of many Britons. But somehow the memory of Carausius survived in Wales. The name, unknown before the emperor, reappears on a tombstone found 4.1km from Penmachno. Dated to the fifth or sixth century, it bears a Latin inscription: 'Here lies Carausius in this pile of stones', below a Christian chi-rho symbol. The emperor also features, in mythologised form, in the work of the later Welsh writers Nennius and Geoffrey of Monmouth.

14. Voteporix stone
c.550 CE

The Roman period came to an end in Britain at the beginning of the fifth century. The conventional date is 410 CE, when the emperor Honorius told the Britons that they could no longer rely on Roman legions to protect them. But the transition to the 'dark ages' that followed was gradual, not sudden. There is little historical or archaeological evidence for the period after around 400 CE – hence the adjective 'dark' – but we do have some traces in Wales that throw suggestive light on post-Roman society.

The Voteporix stone was found in 1895, reused as part of a stile across a churchyard wall at Castell Dwyran, in the far west of Carmarthenshire. It is a volcanic rock and stands about two metres tall. On its face is a circular cross with four arms of equal length, and on one edge is carved a series of notches or short lines. Below the cross are three words: '*MEMORIA VOTEPORIGIS PROTICTORIS*'. Their language is Latin, and the words mean 'the memorial of Voteporix, Protector'. Voteporix is the form of his name in Brythonic, the ancestor of Welsh. The notches are written in an Irish alphabet known as ogham. They give the name as '*Votecorigas*', a form of the Irish 'Votecorix'.

The stone, then, commemorates a man who was clearly a Christian, important enough to deserve a lasting memorial – and an Irishman, or of Irish extraction. The Déisi, a people of south-east Ireland, had been attacking western parts of Wales since the middle of the fourth century, taking advantage of the weakness of Roman rule. In 367 CE they joined the Anglo-Saxons and the Picts in a concerted assault on Britain, known as the Barbarian Conspiracy. Their attacks continued into the fifth century, especially in south-west Wales, where over 60 ogham stones have been found. They settled and founded a dynasty that ruled in the area for several centuries.

Although Voteporix or his forebears had come from Ireland, which had never been part of the Roman empire, he was fully conscious of the Roman heritage of his new country. He chose Latin to appear on his gravestone. '*Protictor*' was a formal title rather than a personal epithet. Originally it was the title given to the emperor's bodyguard, but later it carried a more general, honorific meaning. It is possible that Voteporix had inherited or adopted the title, a sign of his status as a ruler and of the link between his current position and Roman offices of the past. Castell Dwyran stands close to the old Roman road west from Moridunum (Carmarthen), the main Roman fort and town in the area. The stone may have been a wayside monument, and people may have lived on the site continuously since Roman times.

Voteporix lived perhaps as early as the second half of the fifth century. He was a Christian of Irish lineage, but one who identified with the Brythonic culture around him; and a man who was aware of the Roman past (perhaps only three generation ago). But he was also a member of a society that was gradually developing into a new community, Welsh in language – the principality of Dyfed. Only three miles from Castell Dwyran is Narberth, the main court of Dyfed, as we are told in the first sentence of the first of the Mabinogi stories, *Pwyll Prince of Dyfed*.

15 Penannular brooch
8th or 9th century CE

This gold and silver brooch was found in 1991 with the help of a metal detector on Newton Moor, in peaty ground near the river Thaw north of Cowbridge. When they heard of the find, staff of National Museum Wales conducted a survey and excavation. They found that the land had been very boggy and suggested that the brooch was perhaps dropped by accident while its owner was trying to cross the river's floodplain.

The owner, man or woman, was a person of wealth. The brooch's hoop, 51mm in diameter, and pin, used to secure a dress or cloak at the shoulder or breast, are both made of silver, with added gold and filigree ornament. At the centre of each of the rhomboid-shaped terminals, recessed in rectangular frames, is a blue glass bead. This is the only complete silver and gold brooch found so far in Wales, though many bronze versions have come to light; one of them was found in 1993 just 400m away from the silver example. It probably dates to the eighth or ninth century. Penannular brooches are found in Ireland but the Newton Moor brooch is of a type that is characteristically British.

Where might the brooch owner have lived? Few post-Roman settlement sites have been excavated in Wales, but two of them lie not very far from Newton Moor, although they are of earlier date: Hen Gastell at Briton Ferry and, much closer, Dinas Powys.

Hen Gastell was a defended settlement guarding a crossing of the river Nedd. As well as traces of houses, pottery from France and the eastern Mediterranean, glass, beads and amber, stones and metalwork were found, including a penannular brooch of an earlier type than the Newton Moor example. This may be the castle mentioned in later records as the home of Morgan ap Caradog ab Iestyn, the lord of Afan in the twelfth century, but its main period of occupation was between the sixth to the tenth centuries.

The hillfort of Dinas Powys was fortified and occupied between the fifth and seventh centuries. Pottery tableware and storage containers, glass and metalwork were imported, via coastal merchant ships, from Anglo-Saxon England as well as from France and the Mediterranean, and large quantities of animal bones were found, perhaps evidence of large-scale feasting. The excavators found iron slag, crucibles, moulds, fragments of bronze, silver, gold and glass, and a lead die – all signs of metalworking and jewellery manufacture. The Dinas Powys community was quite small, but it may have had close connections with nearby sites, including a monastery established at Llandough.

In this lowland part of Wales at least, then, some people in the post-Roman period lived in or close to well-defended settlements near the coast. Those of high status were far from being culturally isolated or materially poor. Imported goods, including luxuries, point to trading links with Ireland and the Continent, and local industries produced fine metalwork. These centres were dominated by aristocratic leaders whose rule may have been quite local, though they probably owed loyalty to the ruler of a wider area, in this case Glywysing, a kingdom that later became Morgannwg [18]. Through the centuries before the arrival of the Normans the shape and make-up of kingdoms and sub-kingdoms fluctuated continuously, as political power shifted with war and changing alliances.

16 Cadfan stone
8th or 9th century CE

The language most Britons spoke was British or
Brythonic. It had probably evolved continuously since
the Bronze Age or earlier. Brythonic was one of a family
of Celtic languages spoken across many parts of Europe.

In their 350 years of rule the Romans naturally
left a linguistic mark. In lowland Britain Latin became
widely spoken, and in south-east Wales it was probably
the language of at least the elite. Latin affected several
linguistic features of Brythonic. Many Latin words,
especially for aspects of Roman material culture, entered
Brythonic vocabulary. So, Latin pons (bridge) eventually
became modern Welsh pont, taverna (inn) became
tafarn, and ecclesia (church, a Latin borrowing from
Greek) became eglwys.

Stone inscriptions tell us something about the
people of Wales between 400 and 900 CE and their
languages **[14]**. Almost all of them are written in
Latin. This gives the impression that Latin was still
widespread, but in reality it was becoming confined to
special settings, like monasteries and churches, and to a
small range of uses, like stone memorials. As a spoken
language Latin had probably died out by about 700.
Most people in Wales still spoke Brythonic, or Old Welsh,
as it became when Britons in Wales lost contact with
Britons in the north and south west of the island as a
result of Anglo-Saxon settlement in England.

The first and only stone written entirely in Old Welsh
is in Tywyn, Gwynedd. It was found in the churchyard
of St Cadfan's Church. In the early nineteenth century
it had been removed, it was said, 'by a neighbouring
gentleman, to decorate his own grotto', before being
housed inside the church. Its inscription, carved on all
four sides of a pillar standing about 2m high, is hard to
decipher, and interpretations differ. In one reading it may
commemorate four people, including two named women:

> *Tengr(um)ui cimalted gu(reic) Adgan anterunc du*
> *But Marciau*
> Tengrumui wedded wife of Adgan [lies] fairly near
> [*or* very near] to But [and] Marciau [*or* But Marciau]
> *Cun ben Celen, tricet nitanam*
> Cun, woman [or wife] of Celyn, a mortal wound
> remains

Some of the words are recognisable from later Welsh, for
example *gureic* (*gwraig*: woman or wife) and *tricet* (*trigo*:
dwell, stay).

Latest research dates the stone to the eighth or ninth
century. Around the same time we have one of the oldest
surviving manuscripts in the Welsh language. It occurs
in marginal additions to an incomplete vellum copy of
the Gospels, now in Lichfield Cathedral but once in a
church of St Teilo, probably Llandeilo Fawr. The largest
section, known as the Surexit Memorandum, records
the settling of a land dispute by informal compromise:
Elgu promises to give Tudfwlch a horse and cattle, and
Tudfwlch undertakes never to lay claim to the land
again. The Welsh text, expressed in semi-legal language,
is sprinkled with Latin words where the Welsh-speaking
scribe was uncertain about technical terms.

These two fragments are late, rare and mundane.
But the early Welsh language was also a medium for
more sophisticated expression. One of the earliest
surviving poems in Old Welsh, 'Y Gododdin', ascribed
to Aneirin, was composed in the north of England
or southern Scotland, and recalls a military defeat at
'Catraeth' (Catterick in north Yorkshire).

17 St Cystennin's Bell

9th century

Early medieval Wales is sometimes called the Age of the Saints. There was certainly no lack of them. About eighty gave their names to monasteries and churches, as Christianity spread and rooted itself throughout the fluid new kingdoms of the Welsh. Place names beginning 'Llan' (a church and its surrounding land) are usually linked with the name of the 'saint' or patron who settled or gave the land.

Christians were already active in late Roman Wales, and their religious practices and organisation probably survived the end of Roman rule. But Wales was also open to the work of missionaries from Ireland and the Continent as they sailed the Atlantic seaways linking Wales with south-west England, Ireland and elsewhere. Their work was effective, and Wales in turn exported Christian missionaries to Brittany and elsewhere. Within 200 years a patchwork of monasteries, mother churches (*clasau*) and smaller churches covered most of Wales.

Later writers invented and embroidered lives of the saints and legends about them. We know almost nothing about them from the age they lived in, between 400 and 600 CE. Some, like David, Illtud [18] and Padarn, were influential, with several churches named after them in many parts of Wales. Others were local, known only for a single site. One of these was St Cystennin, in whose name a small church was founded near Mochdre. 'Cystennin' is a Welsh version of Constantine, a common name since the Christian Roman emperor Constantine and perhaps a sign of continuity with the Roman past.

Nothing remains of Cystennin's building. An earlier building was demolished in 1843 to make way for a new church – except for a portable bell, discovered by an antiquary and folklorist, Elias Owen, suspended halfway up the gable end of the local school. Fearing for its safety at the hands of the schoolchildren, he deposited it in the Powysland Museum in Welshpool in 1891.

Making hand-bells seems to have been an Irish tradition. Seventy-five survive from Ireland, where carvings show priests carrying them. Nineteen similar bells have been found in Scotland and seven in Wales. They were used for a variety of purposes, including calling the faithful to prayer, in a period before churches had bells hung high in their buildings. Cystennin's bell, about 20cm high, though it has lost its handle and clapper, is in good condition. Its plainness makes it hard to date, but it may have been made in the ninth century. It was cast in solid bronze, a process that called for advanced metalworking techniques.

Handbells were valuable objects. In Ireland some became venerated as the relics of saints and were covered with elaborately decorated shrines. Over the years legends gathered around them. There are stories about Gildas, a fifth-century Welsh monk, making bells and presenting one to the Pope. In the twelfth century Giraldus Cambrensis [19, 42] tells of the miraculous bell of Glascwm in Radnorshire. A woman took the bell, called a 'bangu' and supposed to have belonged to St David, to Rhayader to free her husband from prison. When the gaolers seized her and the bell, God took revenge during the night, burning the whole castle, except the wall on which the bell hung. In the 1890s Elias Owen collected traditions about handbells and their uses – in celebrating mass, preceding funeral processions, marking a person's dying, announcing proclamations and swearing oaths.

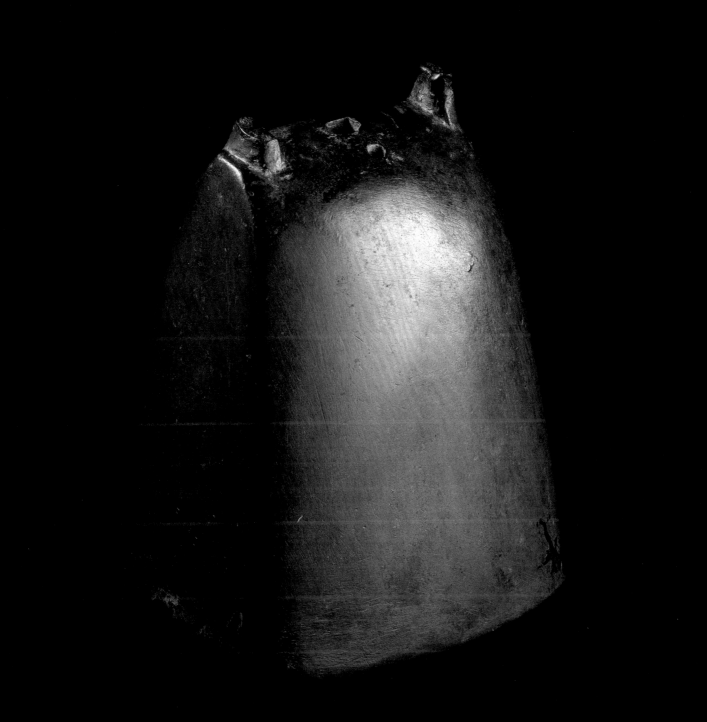

18 Houelt cross

c.850-886 CE

'In the name of God, the Father and the Holy Spirit, Houelt prepared this cross for the soul of Res his father.' Houelt was Hywel ap Rhys, king of Glywysing [15], known from Welsh annals and genealogies. He died in 886 CE. When he decided to order a memorial for his father, with this Latin inscription carved on its base, the choice of location was obvious: the monastery at Llantwit Major, a traditional resting place of local kings.

By tradition St Illtud founded the monastery in the sixth century. Nothing of it now survives – its buildings may have underlain the site of the existing church, which dates to the twelfth century – but the author of a *Life of St Samson* in the seventh or eighth century preserves some of the aura still surrounding the saint:

Of all the Britons Illtud was in truth the most learned in all the scriptures, both the Old and New Testaments, and in every branch of philosophy, poetry and rhetoric, grammar and arithmetic, and all the arts; and he was the wisest sage and prophet. I have been in his splendid monastery and I could say more about his great achievements...

It seems likely that it was Illtud who transplanted the early Christian tradition of monasticism to Wales, and continued the tradition of Latin learning. His influence was wide. The school at Llantwit became famous, exporting its pupils far and wide: St Samson travelled via Cornwall and the Scilly and Channel Islands to Dol in Brittany, where he founded his own monastery. Thirteen other church dedications were made to Illtud in Wales, and others in Brittany. His monastery did not shun the secular world, as Hywel ap Rhys's lavish memorial shows.

Hywel ap Rhys, for all his artistic splendour and large territory, was a king under pressure. In 864 Glywysing was attacked by Anglo-Saxons. Later the kingdom of Mercia [19] threatened from the north-east and Hywel was forced to turn to Alfred the Great, King of Wessex, for protection. Periodic English domination of Welsh lands, often encouraged by Welsh leaders, was to continue up to the loss of Welsh independence.

One of the first people to record the Houelt cross, in 1797, was the stonemason, radical poet, collector and forger Iolo Morganwg [40]. Iolo found it outside a door of the church. At its top is a ring-cross, common in sculptures of the period, with square panels of a diaper pattern in the arm-ends, and triangular knotwork between the arms. Intricate diagonal fretwork covers the shaft. The highly-skilled carver may have been Irish, or at least influenced by Irish masons: there are slabs of similar design from Tullylease, Co. Cork.

Eight early Christian sculptures or fragments are known from Llantwit Major. One of them, the Samson Pillar, was discovered by Iolo Morganwg. According to his own account he remembered that 30 years earlier a local shoemaker had said that an ancient inscribed stone had toppled into the newly dug grave of a man called 'Will the Giant'. The stone proved too heavy to lift and it was buried with the body. In 1789 Iolo excavated the grave and found the stone, with 'the bones of a larger size than usual'. 'We found a fidelity in the tale', wrote Iolo, 'that does great credit to popular tradition' – or possibly to Iolo's imagination.

19 Llangors textile

9th century CE

At the foot of the Black Mountains lies Llyn Syfaddon or Llangorse Lake. About 40m from its north shore is a small, near-circular island, Ynys Bwlc. Sailing past the island in 1867, Edgar Dumbleton noticed a large collection of stones at its edge. Exploring later with his brother Henry, he found over 60 oak slabs lining the island's shore, and on it, charcoal and traces of animal bones and pottery. Realising the island was artificial, he called it a crannog, the Irish term for a lake island dwelling. Crannogs are common in Ireland and Scotland, but this was the first example found in England or Wales.

What the Dumbletons did not guess was that the crannog was a royal centre or *llys* of Brycheiniog, a small Welsh kingdom with links to Ireland and often threatened by its powerful Welsh and English neighbours.

Between 1989 and 1993 teams from National Museum Wales and Cardiff University excavated part of the island. They uncovered a complex wooden and stone structure, along with combs, brooches and pins, a hinge from a portable shrine, carbonised grain, animal bones and signs of metalworking. They dated the wood to around 890 CE. The *llys* probably had a large hall and was connected to the mainland by a wooden causeway. Its inhabitants fished in the lake: a log boat of the period was recovered from the lake bed in 1925.

Traces of burning suggest the settlement came to a sudden end. The *Anglo-Saxon Chronicle* says that in the year 916 CE 'the innocent Abbot Ecgberht was killed, before midsummer … and within three nights Æthelflæd sent an army into Wales, and stormed Brecenanmere [Llangorse]; and there took the king's wife, with some thirty-three others.' Æthelflæd, daughter of Alfred the Great, led the Mercians [19], the dominant Anglo-Saxon military power at the time.

In 1990, in the silt surrounding the crannog, a lump of textile was found, doubly preserved by burning and immersion. In the studio conservators gradually unfolded the blackened bundle, revealing a worn needlework design and allowing the original coloured textile to be reconstructed. Early medieval textiles very rarely survive. The Llangorse fragment, perhaps part of a dress, is remarkable for its superb craftwork. Woven from linen and embroidered with silk and linen (about 25 threads to the centimetre), it shows birds and other animals surrounded by vine leaves, and a border of three-legged lions and other patterns. The silk may have come from Byzantium, and the garment may also have been imported, maybe from England.

In 934 Tewdwr, king of Brycheiniog, is recorded witnessing a document for Æthelstan, Æthelflæd's successor, but Brycheiniog soon ceased to be an independent kingdom. Echoes of the splendour of Llangorse Lake, though, remained. To local people, according to Giraldus Cambrensis [17, 42] in the twelfth century, it sometimes appeared to be 'covered with buildings or rich fields'. In 1801 a verse drama was published called *The Fairy of the Lake*. Its author was John Thelwall, a radical republican and a friend of Samuel Taylor Coleridge, who settled for three years in nearby Llyswen as a retreat from urban politics. The plot, subversively reversing the tide of history, tells how Rowena, an evil Saxon sorceress, is defeated and Arthur restored to the British throne, with the help of the lady of Llangorse Lake (Lynn Savadan).

20 The Laws of Hywel Dda

c.950 CE (manuscript mid-13th century)

The laws of the Welsh kingdoms were different.
Though they share much with the laws of Ireland, many of them were very unlike the laws of the Anglo-Saxons and the later Normans.

The Welsh laws were known as *Cyfraith Hywel*, the Laws of Hywel. Hywel Dda or Hywel the Good, born around 880 CE, inherited the kingdom of Seisyllwg, modern Ceredigion and part of Carmarthenshire. From there he built a much larger kingdom, through luck and astute diplomacy and by taking care to keep good relations with his powerful English neighbours. By 942, eight years before his death, it included all of Wales except the south-east. Whether it was Hywel who codified Welsh law, as tradition says, or whether later generations attributed to him laws that developed over a long period, is still debated. The earliest manuscripts of *Cyfraith Hywel* date from only the thirteenth century and record law dating from that period.

Many of the surviving legal manuscript books were small in format, and used by lawyers in their everyday work, but Peniarth 28, one of the earliest, was a special copy. It is larger, written in Latin, and, very unusually, has illustrations. The drawing of a woman carrying a dish precedes a section about the law relating to women. The Laws of Hywel were more favourable to women than other legal codes of the time. On marriage, half the dowry was due to the woman if the couple separated before the end of seven years. On divorce possessions were divided between the two, the woman keeping 'all the dishes bar one'. If she found her husband with another woman, a wife was entitled to payment on the first two occasions, and on the third she could divorce him. If her husband beat her, in most cases she was entitled to the payment of *sarhad* (insult or injury). In a charge of rape the woman's claim was given precedence.

In general the Laws emphasise the importance of compensation rather than harsh punishment as a remedy for lawbreaking. A fine was the usual sentence, and the death penalty was reserved for serious cases of theft.

Peniarth 28 was once kept in the library of Canterbury Cathedral (it may have been written for English use). In October 1279 John Pecham, Archbishop of Canterbury [24], wrote to Llywelyn ap Gruffudd, the last independent Welsh leader [23], complaining about the 'unbiblical' Laws of Hywel Dda. In November 1282 he wrote again, after Llywelyn rejected his peace terms, attacking him and the Welsh and criticising the Laws for their lax attitude to marriage. In the section on divorce the manuscript has some marks in the margin, possibly made by Pecham himself. The loyalty of the Welsh to their own laws was one of the main bones of contention between Edward I and Llywelyn. Even after the Edwardian conquest the Laws continued to be used in the Marcher Lordships of Wales: most of the forty surviving Welsh law books date from after 1282.

A prologue to some of the manuscripts of the Laws claims that in order to codify Welsh laws Hywel convened a forty-day seminar of representatives from all parts of his kingdom in Hendy-gwyn (Whitland in Carmarthenshire). Most scholars think this unlikely, but today the Laws are remembered in Whitland at the Hywel Dda heritage centre and gardens.

... egalans ...
... ad eut una uice ...
... loues qm subtus factu
plaute ampl' pacans culpand
Sic arma sua si suspendic ab'
sin sic caput hoir eanac. a nea quic
... caput fuit, arma sue uulnauit ut
... reddac. cui fuic dra docil redd

Siqs arma sua accomodauerit
... uulneraueric fuit ut occис
odacum, semp reddac. Sicc
supple ut turpic loquitans
... uacac camur duplicacer
... sedes septe si dm epales
... in cambria. i seuech.
... Egluyse degenman.
... Egluyse dylan, eglu
... kenew. Abbes e
... smaelis e
... ec etia sue ordi
... illor. dno di
... qui illic sue
... eucuia quia
... soluta.

ccl'ia kenew ee eccl'ia b'
... amec abullo debuco lib' eun
... sanguinolentu ecouenui pe
... de gente sua in obp'brium
genu tui. e in memoriam reddic'
Hemo m'euerence anecer'a
... plente ut sint canonicas iudicare p'c
... sunic. De lege puellar e feld'

Siquis ducac uxorem dacam er a
gente sua e infra septennui ea
dimittac, reddac ei suu egredi.
Sin poc septennium dimicac, e
omni substancia deber h'e simul, de
nisi uir p alia lib'tace possit plut
h'e. De ple duas p'es deber uir p'
curare. f maiore e minore. Mac
nero cenia. Si ut uni sui fuuic ult

21 Smalls sword guard
c1100

'852: Cyngen was killed by heathens.'

This entry in the *Annales Cambriae* is the first record of a people new to Wales. Cyngen, presumably a Welsh ruler, is otherwise unknown, but the 'heathens' were certainly Vikings. From about 840 CE Vikings had been sailing between Ireland and the west coast of Britain, raiding and later settling, for example in Dublin and the Isle of Man. Now they turned on Wales. Attacks on north Wales were fought off in 855 and again in 902 or 903, but after the death of Hywel Dda [20] in 950 a second wave of raids began, targeting ecclesiastical sites at Holyhead, Penmon, Clynnog Fawr, Tywyn, Llanbadarn Fawr, St Davids, St Dogmaels, Llantwit Major and Llancarfan. St Davids suffered eleven Viking visits between 967 and 1091.

Until recently little was known about the Scandinavians in Wales, apart from mentions in annals and the evidence of place names. The Welsh annals speak fearfully of attacks by 'pagans' and 'dark Northmen'. Their visits are recalled in the Norse-derived names for islands, including those ending in 'ey' (Anglesey, Bardsey, Caldey) and 'holm' (Priestholm, Grassholm, Skokholm).

In the 1990s excavations by National Museum Wales at Llanbedr-goch near the east coast of Anglesey shed new light on Viking activity. They uncovered a large D-shaped enclosure including a large hall, dating to the ninth and tenth centuries. Around the mid-ninth century it was surrounded by a stone rampart, perhaps to defend against attacks from the sea. Large numbers of objects were found, some showing Irish-Norse influence; in particular silver ingots and hacksilver, and lead weights,

evidence of Viking-age trade. Llanbedr-goch was a busy agricultural, manufacturing and trading settlement, important for the economy of the kingdom of Gwynedd. Its finds show that the Vikings came to Wales not just to seize goods, hostages or slaves, but also to trade and even to settle (as some non-Christian burials there suggest).

In 1991 a diver made a spectacular find while investigating the wreck of the steamship *Rhiwabon*, lost in 1884 on a dangerous reef called The Smalls, 13km west of Grassholm on the Pembrokeshire coast. She found, lodged by accident in the wreck, a richly decorated Viking sword guard. Made of brass and 118mm long, it was densely covered with complex ornament. On each side were two animals in profile, interwoven with thin, snake-like beasts. Strips of silver wire were inlaid in the design, and black niello would have filled the background. The decoration is in the Irish-Norse Urnes style and has parallels in Irish metalwork of the time. The guard can be dated to around 1100-25.

No trace of the rest of the sword was found when the site was inspected. Though the sword, some 90cm long, was a regular Viking weapon, this example was hardly a standard issue. It may have been a ceremonial example, or belonged to a leader. The vessel carrying it – perhaps one of the Vikings' fast longships – may have been wrecked on The Smalls.

Around this time Gruffudd ap Cynan was ruler of Gwynedd, between 1081 and 1107. He was born in Dublin. According to his biographer, his father was Welsh, but his mother, Ragnailt ingen Amlaíb, was the granddaughter of Sigtrygg Silkbeard, a member of the Norse dynasty in Ireland. Gruffudd relied on Irish and Danish military aid to gain the throne of Gwynedd.

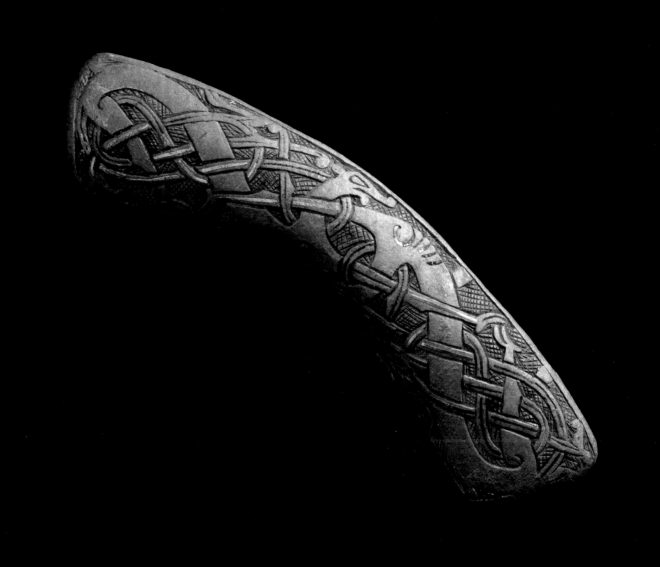

22 Deganwy stone head
Early 13th century

Deganwy today is a suburb of Conwy, but in the period of the Welsh princes the twin-peaked hill above the town was an important military base, commanding the mouth of the river Conwy. It had been the stronghold of Maelgwn Gwynedd, a sixth-century ruler of north Wales. In 1213 Llywelyn ap Iorweth, Llywelyn the Great, built his own castle on the site.

Llywelyn was the most consistently successful of the Welsh rulers. For forty years from 1200 his astute diplomacy and well-directed military force allowed him to tighten his grip on his kingdom, Gwynedd, and extend his power over most of the rest of independent Wales. He made alliances of convenience with English kings, John and Henry III, and with English Marcher lords, but he could overturn them if conflict suited him better than compromise. He married John's daughter, Joan, to guarantee an agreement with the Crown, and later married his own daughters to English lords in south Wales. Until his final years he was often at war with some Welsh or Norman power. Llywelyn's great seal, a symbol of his status and power, shows a mounted warrior wielding a long sword.

Llywelyn was a keen castle builder. Castell y Bere, located on a rocky outcrop in the Dysynni valley and equipped with sophisticated fortifications, gives the best impression of his work. Today little remains of his castle at Deganwy, but in the 1960s archaeologists found traces of its foundations. They also uncovered in a pile of rubble a sandstone carving of a male head.

The stone is in the form of a corbel which probably supported the beams of an internal building – a chapel or a hall in Llywelyn's castle.

The head is in good condition (the original colour has been lost, and the nose restored). It shows a royal ruler, ringlets of bushy hair peeping from under the circular band of his crown. The Romanesque sculpture has a simple frontal composition and a bold, stylised treatment of the large eyes, ears and beard. Possibly this is the face of Llywelyn ap Iorwerth himself – not a strict portrait, more the official image Llywelyn wished to broadcast to visitors: that of a powerful, noble and determined ruler.

So little has survived of the interior of the Welsh rulers' centres, it is tempting to believe that they were crude, unadorned places. But the Deganwy head, and the finely-carved stone fragments found in some of Llywelyn's other castles, at Cricieth and Castell y Bere, suggest that architects and artists were as welcome at the royal court as the poets who praised the exploits of the king and mourned his death when it finally came in 1240, in his bed, in the Cistercian abbey of Aberconwy.

An illustration in a manuscript now in Cambridge shows the dying Llywelyn with his grieving sons, Gruffydd and Dafydd. After his death they fell out and Henry III took advantage of their split. Never again was Wales to be united under a single ruler.

Seal of Llywelyn ap Iorwerth from Strata Marcella Abbey (National Library of Wales)

23 Cara Wallia derelicta
1959 (commemorating 1282)

For many in Wales 11 December 1282 marked the end of the world. On that date Llywelyn ap Gruffudd, the last independent Welsh ruler, was killed in an ambush by English soldiers near Builth Wells.

Llywelyn, the grandson of Llywelyn ap Iorwerth [22], came to the throne of Gwynedd on the death of his uncle Dafydd in 1246. At first he had success in dominating his Welsh competitors and withstanding the English king. The treaty he signed with Henry III at Montgomery in 1267 confirmed his rule over north Wales and Brycheiniog and gave him the title, never before used, Prince of Wales. But he soon clashed with the Marcher lords, with members of his own family, and finally with the new King, Edward I. After a military invasion by Edward, Llywelyn was forced to sign a new treaty at Aberconwy, which reduced his territory to the western part of Gwynedd. Discontent with Edward's rule led to an uprising in 1282, led by Llywelyn's brother Dafydd. Llywelyn eventually joined the revolt. He was trying to open a new front against Edward's forces in mid-Wales when he was killed, in mysterious circumstances, on 11 December.

In 1959 the poet and artist David Jones painted 'Cara Wallia derelicta' ('Dear Wales abandoned') to commemorate the disaster. His inscription interweaves two languages, Latin and Welsh, and three quotations: an entry for the date of Llywelyn's death from the Welsh chronicle *Brenhinedd y Saesson* ('then all Wales was hurled to the ground'), lines from the Roman poet Virgil about an earlier catastrophe, the fall of Troy ('then came Troy's final day and its inescapable doom'), and parts of a famous Welsh poem, the elegy for Llywelyn written shortly after his death by Gruffudd ab yr Ynad Coch.

Gruffudd's long poem sees Llywelyn's death as the complete end of the Wales he knows. Its repetitive language and rhythms hammer home the terrible, inconsolable loss, both personal and communal. David Jones chose two extracts: 'There is no counsel, no lock, no opening', and 'A lord's head, a dragon's head was on him, / head of fair Llywelyn; the world shivers with fright / that an iron stake should pierce it.' Llywelyn's body was buried in Abbey Cwmhir, but Edward had his head removed and displayed, mockingly crowned with ivy, on a pole in the Tower of London. Welsh resistance continued for a few months, before Edward occupied the old kingdom, subjected it to his direct rule, and encircled it with an arc of massive stone castles.

Not everyone in Wales mourned Llywelyn, and most people were preoccupied with coming to terms with the new English rule. For several centuries Llywelyn's name almost vanished from recollection. Then the rise of national Welsh consciousness, at the turn of the nineteenth century and again in the second half of the twentieth century, found a new use for his memory. An obelisk was erected in 1902 at Cilmeri to commemorate Llywelyn's death; William Goscombe John [68] created a Llywelyn medal, and in 1916 Henry Pegram carved a statue of him for Cardiff City Hall. After David Jones's commemoration the composer William Mathias wrote 'Elegy for a Prince', for baritone and orchestra, in 1972, and Gerallt Lloyd Owen published his famous poem 'Cilmeri' in 1982. Historians too finally gave due attention to the first and last native Prince of Wales.

cara·Wallia·derelicta

ÐVGWYL·DAMASEVS
BABYRVNVED·DYÐAR
ÐEG·OVIS·RAGFYR
DVW·GWENER+
ACYNA·I·BWRIWYD
HOIL·GYMRY
YR·ILAWR. VENIT·SVMMA·DIES
ET·INELVCTABILE·TEMPVS
DARDANIÆ. PENN·DRAGON
PENN·DREIC·OED·ARNAW
PENN·ILYWELYN·DEG
DYGYN·A·VRAW·BYT·BOT
PAWL·HAEARN·TRWYDAW.
ab·hieme·añ·1282

NYT·OES·NA·XYN·GOR·NA·XLO·NAC·EGOR.

24. Corbel from Haverfordwest Priory

14th or 15th century

The Welsh had long had their own enclosed religious communities **[18]**. The Normans brought with them a different monastic model, based on orders of monks founded on the Continent. These planted daughter houses, both monasteries and nunneries – at first in Norman-governed parts of Wales and then in Welsh-ruled areas. The Cistercians, or White Monks, settled at fifteen sites given to them by Welsh rulers, including Abbey Cwmhir, Cymer and Strata Florida. The monks played an important part in the spiritual, economic and cultural life of their patrons **[26]**.

Another order, the Augustinians or Black Canons, settled at nine locations in Wales, starting with Llanthony. Around 1200 Robert FitzRichard, Norman lord of Haverfordwest, founded an Augustinian priory on the banks of the river Cleddau outside the walled town, which had prospered since its foundation some 70 years earlier. The remains of the priory survive. It followed the usual monastery plan: a cruciform church with a tower, chapter house, dormitory, refectory and other service buildings. Between the priory and the river lay a formal garden, with rectangular raised beds surrounded by paved walkways – a rare example of an ecclesiastical garden surviving from medieval Britain. About 13 canons lived in the priory at its zenith. They earned income from their properties in the town and parish churches they served, including those at Dale, Camrose and St Ishmaels.

After the defeat of Llywelyn ap Gruffudd, John Pecham, Archbishop of Canterbury **[20]**, made a tour of Wales to assert his authority over the Welsh church. On his visit to Haverfordwest Priory in 1284 he criticised the prior, like a modern auditor, for minor financial irregularities, and urged him to spend more time mixing with the canons and less time entertaining guests.

The priory was small, but not poor. Donations from benefactors funded the addition of a tower on the church and fitting the rectangular chapter house with a new ribbed vault, decorated plaster walls, and green and buff floor tiles. In the middle of the room stood a plinth supporting the limestone effigy of a man in chain mail. Since the style is thirteenth-century, he may be the priory's founder, or a member of his family. Another well-preserved fragment recovered from excavation is a carved corbel supporting the vault. It is an unusual sculpture, showing seven male faces, of varying degrees of unattractiveness. Each shares an eye with his neighbour. The heads may be images of the Seven Deadly Sins, a common theme in church wall paintings of the time **[28]**.

By the time it was closed in 1537 following Henry VIII's dissolution of the monasteries the priory had declined and housed only four canons and the prior. The site was bought from the Crown by Richard and Thomas Barlow, brothers of the Bishop of St Davids. Stone, lead and other materials were later removed from the priory buildings. The local magnate Sir John Perrot **[37]** may have used some of the stone to repair his nearby house at Haroldston.

Effigy of a knight from Haverfordwest Priory (Haverfordwest Town Museum)

25 The arms of Owain Glyndŵr
c.1405

Llywelyn ap Gruffudd's defeat [23] did not end discontent and antagonism felt towards to English rule in Wales. Tensions were worsened by legal discrimination, extortionate taxation and economic hardship. What began as a local dispute between Owain Glyndŵr and Reginald Grey, Lord of Ruthin, turned rapidly into a ten-year revolt engulfing most of Wales.

Owain Glyndŵr was an unlikely rebel. A landowner in Glyndyfrdwy and Sycharth, near the English border, he had served in the army of Richard II. But for reasons that are unclear he saw himself in 1400 as the leader of a wider, all-Wales revolt. On 16 September he declared himself 'Prince of Wales' and gathered a band to attack English towns in north-east Wales. The king's forces quickly suppressed the uprising, but in April 1401 the undefeated rebels captured Conwy Castle, sparking attacks across Wales. Using guerrilla strikes as well as set-piece battles, Glyndŵr and his men got the better of English forces until by 1403 the revolt was national in scale.

After a two-year siege Harlech Castle fell to Glyndŵr by the end of 1404. He treated it as his headquarters, installed his family, and in August 1405 held his second parliament there. In 1923 workmen uncovered in the castle a roundel, 40mm in diameter, made of copper alloy. Holes in flanges around its edge attached the mount to a belt or harness. Inside the circular frame is a shield of arms, in green and black enamel with gold overlay – the arms of Owain Glyndŵr. The mount may have belonged to Glyndŵr himself or one of his circle. The same arms appear on the great seal on a letter he sent from Pennal in March 1406 to Charles VI, King of France, asking for his help. Glyndŵr's borrowing of the four lions rampant from the arms of Gwynedd shows his skill in legitimising his cause. He had other methods of self-promotion. Prophecies were used to herald his coming. The poets of his court, like Iolo Goch, sang his praises. His advisers surrounded him with the trappings of royal status.

The Pennal letter reveals that Glyndŵr held an unusually strategic, long-term vision. His programme for a new Wales included the establishment of two universities, and the restoration of the ecclesiastical province of Wales, centred on St Davids.

Glyndŵr was never challenged or betrayed. Yet he was finally unable to defeat the superior forces of the English. In February 1409 Harlech Castle was recaptured after a siege, the revolt faded, and Glyndŵr vanished.

His name, however, was never forgotten. In the eighteenth century the poet Evan Evans and the writer Thomas Pennant treated Glyndŵr as a major and heroic figure. In October 1916 a sculpture of him was unveiled in Cardiff City Hall [23]. The artist, Alfred Turner, who specialised in images of Queen Victoria, now celebrated a Welsh rebel. The unveiler, David Lloyd George, once a rebel himself, was about to become the wartime British Prime Minister.

Statue of Owain Glyndŵr (Cardiff City Hall)

26 The Nanteos Cup
Late medieval period

In August 1878 members of the Cambrian
Archaeological Association held their summer meeting
in Lampeter. In a temporary exhibition there they were
shown a plain and fragmentary, but unusual object.
According to the association's president, it was 'a
wooden bowl, preserved for many years past at Nanteos,
and most kindly placed at our disposal by the present
owner of that mansion and estate. It is supposed to have
been a possession of the abbey of Strata Florida ... In
the days of my youth, and probably long since, it was
supposed to possess healing powers which could only
be called miraculous'. These powers, he added, stemmed
from the belief that the bowl had formed part of the
True Cross.

The wooden bowl, made from wych elm and
originally around 12cm in diameter, came to be known
as the Nanteos Cup. The report to the Cambrians
is the first surviving account of it. But some earlier
handwritten receipts exist recording the loan of the
vessel. One of them reads, '27th November 1857: cup
lent this day to Mr Wm Rowland, Ystrad, Tregaron, for
the use of his sister Mrs Jones, Maesllyn, left £1.0.0;
wholly cured and the cup returned 2nd January.' The
receipts confirm that the Cup was popularly believed to
have the power of curing diseases, especially in women.

The 'present owner' was George Powell, who had
just inherited the house and estate of Nanteos, near
Aberystwyth. He was an eccentric member of the
gentry who had dominated Welsh rural society for three
centuries. Never in need of money, he spent much of
his short life travelling abroad, collecting art and books,
befriending the poet Algernon Charles Swinburne,
idolising Richard Wagner, and promoting Icelandic
literature. According to the writer Guy de Maupassant,
'he loved the supernatural, the macabre, the tortured,
the intricate and every form of derangement'.

Strata Florida abbey, near Pontrhydfendigaid, was
founded by the Cistercians in 1164 **[24]**. As well as being
large landowners, the monks were energetic supporters
of the native Welsh kingdoms and their culture. During
Owain Glyndŵr's uprising **[25]** they were suspected by
English forces of siding with Glyndŵr and for a time
were evicted from the abbey.

In 1888 the excavator of Strata Florida, Stephen
W. Williams, suggested that the Nanteos Cup came
from the abbey and was a medieval mazer – a shallow,
handle-less wooden drinking vessel, with a broad lip
of gold or silver fastened to the rim. Mazers were once
common in churches and monasteries (the only other
known Welsh example, dating from the late fifteenth
century, comes from Clynnog church). The rim of the
Nanteos Cup is carved to receive a metal band, and its
foot-stand probably once had a metal flange attached.

Possibly, then, the Cup was once used, in connection
with a holy well known to exist at Strata Florida, until the
abbey's dissolution in 1539. Then it may have passed to
John Stedman, who acquired the estate around 1560,
and then to the Powells of Nanteos, who owned the land
from 1745. In the absence of direct evidence, though, it
is equally possible that the link with Strata Florida is a
myth. In the early twentieth century the Cup gained a
new myth – that it was the true Holy Grail. It was lent to
the National Library of Wales in 2016.

27 Jesse carving
Late 15th century

In Norman times St Mary's church in Abergavenny belonged to a Benedictine priory. It was a large and rich foundation, patronised by the powerful Hastings, de Braose and Herbert families. Their sumptuous effigies and tombs can still be seen in the church. Towards the end of the fifteenth century a benefactor commissioned a woodcarver to create a sculpture for the church. Only the lowest part of the work survives. The art historian Andrew Graham-Dixon described it as 'the only great wooden figure to survive the wreckage of the British cultural revolution' during the Reformation.

The sculpture was an unusually large and ornate example of a Jesse tree, a visual way of explaining how Christ was descended, through his mother Mary, from King David and his father, Jesse, as the prophet Isaiah foretold: 'and there shall come forth a rod out of the stem of Jesse, and a branch shall grow out of his roots'. The Jesse tree became popular in the late Middle Ages. In Wales it appears in stone sculptures, and in stained glass windows in three churches in north-east Wales, including Llanrhaeadr-yng-Nghinmeirch in Denbighshire.

The Abergavenny Jesse was carved using a single section of oak, from a tree already perhaps 400 years old. The underside is flat and may have rested on a plinth, while original nails indicate that the sculpture was fixed at the back to a wall or framework. Jesse lies on his right side, an old man with long hair and beard, and wearing a hat. An angel holds a cushion supporting his head. A mantle covers his shoulder, flows beneath him and envelops the lower part of his body. Originally the figure was brightly painted: red, black and gold for the mantle, pink for Jesse's flesh, gold for the angel's hair.

There was no standard pattern for Jesse trees, but the Llanrhaeadr window, which survives almost complete, shows what might have sprung from the root emerging from Jesse's wooden abdomen: David and Solomon, prophets, kings, and, at the top, the Madonna and child. The complete sculpture probably extended some 9m towards the roof of the church. To judge from the confident and expressive carving of the Jesse figure, the unknown sculptor was an accomplished artist, possibly of local origin.

So costly a work could only have been commissioned by a wealthy, well-connected individual. A likely candidate is Jasper Tudor, uncle and mentor of Henry VII [33]. He was lord of Abergavenny and a benefactor of St Mary's. His commission may have had a political purpose. Genealogy, the essence of the Jesse tree, was important to the new Tudor dynasty, eager to end the Wars of the Roses and legitimise Henry's right to rule by appeal to his royal lineage.

St Mary's link with the dynasty proved a blessing later, when Henry VIII ordered the dissolution of the monasteries. In 1536 the burgesses of Abergavenny successfully pleaded with the king that the priory church should not be destroyed, but instead adopted as their parish church.

Jesse window (St Dyfnog's Church, Llanrhaeadr-yng-Nghinmeirch)

28 Death and the young man
15th century

Today white is the predominant colour inside most churches in Wales. But, before the Protestant revolution rejected visual images as a superstitious distraction from the biblical word of God, church walls were like a modern cinema. Worshippers, most of them illiterate, were surrounded by vivid, colourful scenes illustrating Christian truths and the perils of departing from them.

In 2007, during repairs to the roof timbers of St Cadoc's church in Llancarfan in the Vale of Glamorgan, fragments of red ochre paint appeared beneath limewash covering a wall of the south aisle. Conservators removed over twenty coats of limewash to uncover paintings dating from about the mid-fifteenth century – among the best and most complete of their kind yet found in Britain. Discovering them, in the words of the specialist Jane Rutherford, is 'what we conservators of wall paintings dream about.'

One scene shows St George fighting the dragon, watched by a princess and by her anxious parents standing on the battlements of a castle. A second sequence, by the same artist, features the Seven Deadly Sins [24] – 'deadly' because embracing them could condemn one to eternal damnation. Both paintings are very rare, in the way they treat their subjects and in being so complete.

The third scene, by a different artist of the same period, is also unusual. It warns the congregation that death awaits all, however proud, young or wealthy. A long-haired posh boy wearing a chequered puffer jacket, tight leggings, knitted Monmouth cap and sword, looks nervous. He has good reason. His left hand is gripped by a grinning skeletal figure that stands enveloped by the transparent folds of a shroud knotted above its head. This is Death. It pulls the youth aside to usher him away from the world of the living.

This motif, 'Death and the Gallant', is a rare survival in British medieval painting. It was connected to the *danse macabre* or dance of death. Its intention was to remind viewers of the dangers of pride and of the vanity of earthly existence. Death the equaliser was a familiar figure to contemporaries. Their lives were often short, and memories were still fresh of the devastating plague or Black Death of the preceding century.

Another transparent figure appears in the slightly later Mostyn Medical Manuscript, written by Gutun Owain. Gutun, from Dudleston in Shropshire, was a poet and genealogist – his writings were used by the commission Henry VII appointed to trace the genealogy of his grandfather Owain Tudur [27]. Gutun's zodiac man is a diagram explaining how the stars and planets have different effects on parts of the human body and its humours. Aries the ram, for example, was said to have a particular influence on the head; Pisces the fish, on the feet. During the next century Gutun's traditional concepts of medicine would change, just as the wall paintings of Llancarfan, following a royal decree of 1547 ordering the 'obliteration and destruction of popish and superstitious books and images', would vanish under limewash for 450 years.

Gutun Owain's 'zodiac man' (National Library of Wales)

29 Buckler
16th century

War was endemic in medieval Wales. Conflicts between and within kingdoms were common, and Welshmen were often involved in campaigns in other parts of Britain and overseas. After 1485 the Tudor regime brought greater stability, but the demand for arms and armour did not cease. One of the centres of the arms industry in Wales was the area around Wrexham and Ruabon, which specialised in making bucklers.

A buckler was a small, usually circular hand-held iron shield, used in combination with a sword in hand-to-hand combat. In May 1799 an example was found within the Roman fort of Caerhun in the Conwy valley (until 1931 it was thought to be Roman or ancient British). It is circular, 33cm in diameter, and made from hardened leather and an overlapping series of seven concentric iron rings, held together with ball-headed brass rivets. To the opponent the surface appeared convex. A large onion-shaped boss projects from its centre. At the back would have been a wooden handle, secured by iron bands, and in the centre was a piece of coarse hair for padding at the back of the hand. The iron rings of bucklers were originally covered with tin, so that they shone brightly.

Bucklers were no defence against arrows, but were flexible and manoeuvrable in one-to-one combat. They could be used defensively, to deflect sword blows, and in attack to pin down the opponent's limbs. Many were finely made and expensive. They were therefore highly valued, and presented as gifts. Bucklers are often mentioned by poets employed by leading noblemen ('beirdd yr uchelwyr'). Tudur Aled sings in praise of a recently deceased buckler maker from Ruabon, Ieuan ap Deicws, 'master of the backsmith's art, prime creator in steel and fire'. A document of 1472 records that Ieuan was granted a lease to extract ironstone on Ruabon Mountain, presumably used in his forge. Guto'r Glyn **[30, 33]** likens an ornate buckler, a present from Dafydd ap Ieuan, abbot of Vale Crucis, to a moon, wheel, mirror and dish. He sings of its radiating ribs and metal nails:

> Arms from its heart stretch to their ends,
> Rays from the sun; and nails set in ranks:
> Every hammer hits a perfect note, score
> For a song in the workshop of Wrexham.

The historian John Leland **[32]** visited Wrexham in the late 1530s and reported that the town contained 'sum marchauntes and good bokeler makers'. In 1529 Geoffrey Bromefield from the Ruabon area was paid 20s for a buckler which was given to the king, Henry VIII, as a present. By 1531 he was described as 'the kinges boucler maker', and an inventory of Henry's possessions in 1547 listed 'twoo wreckesham Buckelers'. Research has shown that many surviving bucklers were made in and around Wrexham, which developed a reputation for producing high-quality examples.

But bucklers and the industry that produced them were soon obsolete. William Lambarde wrote in the 1580s: 'it has been in times past famous for making bucklers, but since bucklers be grown to targets, Wrexham has lost both the gain and name of that workmanship'. But north-east Wales has remained a centre for the arms industry. In the Second World War Wrexham housed a large ordnance factory. Today the area specialises in military aircraft and technologically advanced systems for controlling them.

30 Raglan gold ring
c.1450-1475

In the fifteenth century, as now, finger rings were given as tokens of love. Few were as large, ornate and expensive as the gold signet ring found by metal detector near Raglan Castle in 1998.

The ring is so large, 22mm in internal diameter, that it may have been intended to be worn over a glove. Its surface is richly decorated with leaves, stems and flowers. The round bezel shows a lion *passant*, standing on flowers and surrounded by the motto, '*to yow feythfoull*' (or '*feythfoull to yow*'). Comparisons with similar gold rings suggest that the Raglan example dates from around 1450 to 1475.

A clue to the identity of the ring's owner, clearly a person of exceptional wealth, is two initials carved on either side of the lion, 'W' and 'A'. Assuming that the find location is not accidental, one researcher has suggested that they might stand for William and Anne – William Herbert, first Earl of Pembroke, and his wife Anne Devereux, who lived at Raglan Castle. A lion appears on Herbert's coat of arms, visible in a manuscript picture of him kneeling with Anne beside the king. The motto's expression of fidelity may refer not only to the couple's vows, but also to William's loyalty to the king.

William Herbert (c1423-1469) was the son of William ap Thomas and Gwladys ferch Dafydd Gam. The father supported Richard, Duke of York, in the Wars of the Roses and built Raglan Castle. The son, brought up in the castle, followed in his footsteps, but surpassed him in political achievement and wealth. In 1461 Edward IV recognised his military support in the Wars of the Roses by giving him the title Baron Herbert of Raglan, and in 1469 the additional honour of Earl of

Pembroke. Herbert remodelled Raglan Castle and its parkland, orchards and fishponds in grand style. His loyalty to the throne gave him control of large parts of Wales. It also led to his downfall. In 1469 Richard Neville, Earl of Warwick, rebelled against the king, defeated Herbert and his partly Welsh army at the battle of Edgecote in Northamptonshire, captured him and put him to death.

Born shortly after Owain Glyndŵr's death, Herbert was one of many Welshmen who calculated that closeness to English power, rather than antagonism to it, was the path to success. He was the first Welshman to become an English peer, anglicising his name and earning from the poet Lewys Glyn Cothi the epithet 'King Edward's master lock', a sign that he had secured Wales for the Crown. He was a patron of other Welsh poets, including Guto'r Glyn [29, 33], who mourned his death:

> Raglan was a vineyard for the people,
> Pity him who will never see its wine again.

Anne Devereux married Herbert in 1449. She came from a powerful Herefordshire family, and the family alliance enabled Herbert to extend his influence into England. They had ten children. From 1461 Anne, 'so eminent was her virtue and prudence', cared for a ward, the young Henry Tudor. Herbert planned in his will, which also mentions a ring, that Henry should marry their daughter Maud. It was Henry who in 1485 returned from exile through Wales to defeat Richard III at Bosworth Field and end the long civil wars. The Yorkist cause, like the ring, was buried.

31 Misericords
c.1500-1510

At the core of the medieval church was the choir, where the monks or clergy prayed. They occupied sets of wooden stalls facing each other, and throughout the service they would stand. Those who were old or infirm, though, were allowed to rest on a small ledge on the underside of the seat behind them. These seats were called misericords, after the Latin word for 'mercy', and underneath them were sometimes carved small wooden figures. St Davids Cathedral has twenty-one, one of the largest series in Britain.

A folk dance is in full swing. Two short men, back to back, are stomping to the music of an unseen band. They lean forward, hands on hips, clogged feet in the air. They wear short tunics and caps cover their heads. Above this little scene is painted the title of the person who occupied this stall, the succentor or under-singer. His music, sacred and formal, was very different from that of the dancers, mirroring the icons of the saints and other holy figures that surrounded him in the cathedral. Yet while these sacred images were targeted for destruction by the Protestant iconoclasts of the reformation and the Civil War, the secular sculptures of the dancers escaped.

Two misericords feature ships and boats. In one, two men are building or repairing a cargo ship. Such vessels, like the fifteenth century ship discovered in Newport in 2002, regularly sailed the Welsh coast. Our ship has a hull of clinker construction, using overlapping planks, and castles at bow and stern. One of the workers hammers a wooden peg into a plank; the other, on his tea break, drinks from a bowl. In the second, men are

at sea in a small boat in rough weather. The oarsman struggles to make progress. Two others comfort a fourth man being sick over the boat's side. This image could tell the story of St Govan, who was almost fatally seasick on a voyage to Rome. However, the exact significance of many misericord images is now lost.

Especially mysterious is the green man. Leaves sprout from the teeth of a grim-looking man or mask, encircling his head. It is an image common in medieval art and is sometimes said, though without evidence, to derive from pre-Christian belief. The same sculptor was responsible for a woman's head. She wears a broad head-dress, a veil and a gap-toothed grimace.

Animals are a common theme in the misericords of St Davids. They may have been taken from bestiaries, manuscripts or printed books of real and imaginary beasts, and often derive from folk tales. In one scene, five pigs attack a fox, a reversal of a common fable. Two intertwined serpents are equipped with ears, which they block to avoid the enchantment of music. A dragon, a symbol of Satan, has his tail pinned, showing that he was been defeated. In an unusual scene, a goose gives a treat of food and drink to a fox wearing a bishop's mitre – perhaps a satire on the sexual mores of the clergy or a warning about temptresses.

Bishop Robert Tully began remodelling the choir of the cathedral in the 1470s, and it is likely that the misericords were carved, each from a single oak block by itinerant woodworkers, in the early years of the sixteenth century.

32 Denbigh borough charter
1506

Many towns in Wales started as Norman or English settlements. The invaders intended them to support their new military bases and to cement their political and economic power in the surrounding areas. Denbigh was no exception. Unusually, a long series of documents survives to show how the town developed over its early centuries.

After Edward I's conquest of Wales the area around Denbigh, the largest lordship of north-east Wales, was granted in October 1282 to Henry de Lacy, Earl of Lincoln and a close adviser to Edward I. Almost immediately de Lacy built a castle on the hilltop in Denbigh, probably on the site of an earlier Welsh stronghold, and then established a town nearby. In 1285 the town was granted a charter. Written in Norman French, it gave 63 burgesses tenancies of land or burgages, together with certain privileges, including the right to trade and enjoy exemptions from tolls and taxes, in exchange for rents and military service in defence of the castle and town. A detailed survey of revenues of the honour of Denbigh in 1334 reveals how legal and tax systems were used to benefit English settlers at the expense of the native Welsh, who were often deprived of their lands and resettled in more remote areas.

A second, undated charter was necessary, marking a re-launch of the town. Growth was slow at first, probably because of periodic unrest among the resentful Welsh population. In 1345 the burgesses complained 'that they were afraid to leave their town and proceed with their daily occupations in case of being plundered and slain ... the Welsh have never since the conquest been so disposed as they are now to rise up'. In 1305 there were 235 burgages, and by 1373 a total of 438. The 1334 survey talks of those who lived within the walls, an area of over nine acres, and those who lived outside (53 acres); in 1476 four times as many burgages lay outside than in. Once the Wars of the Roses were over more peaceful conditions allowed growth to resume. When John Leland **[29]** visited in the 1530s he noticed that Denbigh was 'plentiful of corn and gresse'. It became famous later for its glovers and mercers.

Denbigh's charters had been regularly reviewed and confirmed. In 1506, over twenty years after seizing the throne, Henry VII granted yet another – one of a series of royal charters he issued in north Wales. He modifed the colonial imperialism of Edward I by adding to the rights of the Welsh population. For example he allowed the Welsh to acquire land in England and in English towns in Wales. But by 1536, when Denbigh became the new county town of Denbighshire following the Act of Union, it still showed its origins as a colonial settlement: few borough offices were held by native Welshmen.

The 1506 charter is a large, elaborate and expensive document (Henry VII probably sold it rather than donated it to the town). Written in Latin on parchment, it carries the royal seal to guarantee its authenticity. The text begins with the coloured initial 'H', showing Henry enthroned, holding an orb and sceptre and flanked by his courtiers. In the left-hand margin are two of his badges, a double red rose and the portcullis. The charter stands as a symbol of the majesty and power of the Crown.

33 Effigy of Sir Rhys ap Thomas
After 1525

When Henry Tudor challenged for the throne of England Welsh poets were roused to prophesy. Some foretold a new age for Wales. Henry, born in Pembroke and grandson of a Welshman, would restore the rights and fortunes of their ancient nation. In fact Henry's loyalty to Wales and its people was limited. But there were exceptions, the most conspicuous being Sir Rhys ap Thomas.

Rhys's parents came from modest estates in Carmarthenshire. At first he aligned himself uneasily with Richard III. But when Henry Tudor landed in 1485 at Mill Bay in Pembrokeshire, Rhys calculated that he had more to gain from siding with the rebel than with Richard. Already a seasoned soldier, he gathered an army, joined Henry, and helped defeat Richard at the Battle of Bosworth.

When a skeleton attributed to Richard was unearthed in a Leicester car park in 2012, a large hole was found in the back of its skull. The fatal blow was reportedly dealt by a Welsh soldier with a halberd or long-handled axe. The weapon appears, between two fighting horsemen, possibly Richard and Rhys, in a scene of the battle carved on a panel of a large oak bed commissioned by Rhys around 1507. In a praise-poem written shortly after the battle Guto'r Glyn **[29, 30]** says that Henry 'slew the boar [Richard] and shaved his head, and Sir Rhys like the stars of a shield, with the spear among them on a great horse'. Rhys's loyalty to Henry and his son, Henry VIII, continued: he helped suppress rebels and pretenders threatening royal rule, and fought for the king in France. His reward was a succession of titles and offices. He became the most powerful figure in Wales after the king's uncle, Jasper Tudor **[27]**.

On Rhys's death in 1525 a sumptuous stone monument was erected to his memory in Greyfriars friary in Carmarthen (it was later moved to St Peter's Church). On an elaborate rectangular base lies an effigy of him as martial victor, clad in armour and an overcoat, with his helmet above his head. He wears the robes and insignia of a Knight of the Garter. The context may be the extravagant tournament Rhys arranged in April 1506 to mark the award of the Garter. This five-day event, where Rhys appeared in 'faire gilt armour, on a goodlie steed', was staged at his main residence, Carew Castle, which he had recently transformed from a fortress into a modern palace.

Alongside Rhys lies another figure. She has been identified as one of Rhys's two wives, but the effigy is much smaller in scale than his: it was probably carved on another occasion, and may not represent either wife.

Rhys ap Thomas was not a hero to all. According to the chronicler Elis Gruffudd, 'No common people owned land within twenty miles from a dwelling of old Sir Rhys son of Thomas; if he desired such lands he would appropriate them without payment or thanks, and the disinherited doubtless cursed him.'

Sir Rhys ap Thomas's bed
(Amgueddfa Cymru - National Museum Wales)

34. Grant of Ewenny Priory by Henry VIII
1545

Henry VIII's break with the Pope in 1535, combined with his urgent need for cash, led him the following year to decide to close the country's monasteries and appropriate their wealth. The monasteries of Wales had long been in decline. By 1536 Ewenny Priory, a Benedictine house established as a daughter foundation of St Peter's, Gloucester, in the twelfth century, contained only a prior and two monks. According to a valuation, £78 14s was its meagre annual income. On 28 February 1536 Sir Edward Carne leased the priory and its possessions from Gloucester Abbey for 99 years, at an annual rent of £20 10s. In return he agreed to provide accommodation and a salary to the prior, Edmund Wooton, and his two monks, and even agreed to pay for their successors.

Carne could claim descent from the princes of Gwent, but he belonged to a new class of educated Welsh gentry. Graduating in law from the University of Oxford, he began in the 1530s a long career as a diplomat in Italy, France and the Netherlands. His political skills equipped him to serve very different masters. He helped Henry in his struggles with Rome and his complex marriage negotiations, taking care to keep close to Thomas Cromwell. But he was also active in supporting Mary I in her attempt to restore Catholicism, and acted as her ambassador to the Holy See. In 1559, after the Protestant Elizabeth I came to the throne, he was recalled, but found excuses to remain in Rome, saying that the Pope had forbidden him to leave.

Carne was an expert temporiser but he was also a religious conservative, like many in Wales, and, despite his appointment as a commissioner for the suppression of monasteries, a reluctant reformer. It may be that his unusual leasing arrangement was intended to allow Ewenny Priory to survive as a working monastery. If so, the plan failed, because the prior and his monks were expelled from Ewenny on 2 January 1540. Five years later Carne gained a grant from Henry VIII to purchase the Priory outright, along with other possessions of Gloucester Abbey in the lordship of Ogmore, for the price of £727 6s 4d. Later he built a 'goodly house' or mansion within the grounds of the old priory.

The 1545 grant is written in Latin on a large parchment document carrying Henry's great seal. At the start of the text is an illustration showing the king seated on a throne labelled '*Vivat Rex*' and holding his sceptre and orb, according to the common formula **[32]**. The drawing was probably intended to be worked up in full colour. It is a cartoon version of the fifty-four-year-old king: his bulbous head is dominated by an untidy beard covering his large jowls.

Sir Edward Carne died in Rome in 1561. Despite his Catholic leanings – his family continued to be recusants for several generations – his estates passed safely to his son Thomas. Thomas was a litigious and violent man who consolidated the family's power: he was elected as an MP twice, and was High Sheriff of Glamorgan three times. The mansion was extended and later rebuilt on a grander scale. The Carnes, and their successors by marriage the Turbervills, were typical of a small number of families who, through their large estates and inherited wealth, dominated the political and economic life of Glamorgan for centuries to come.

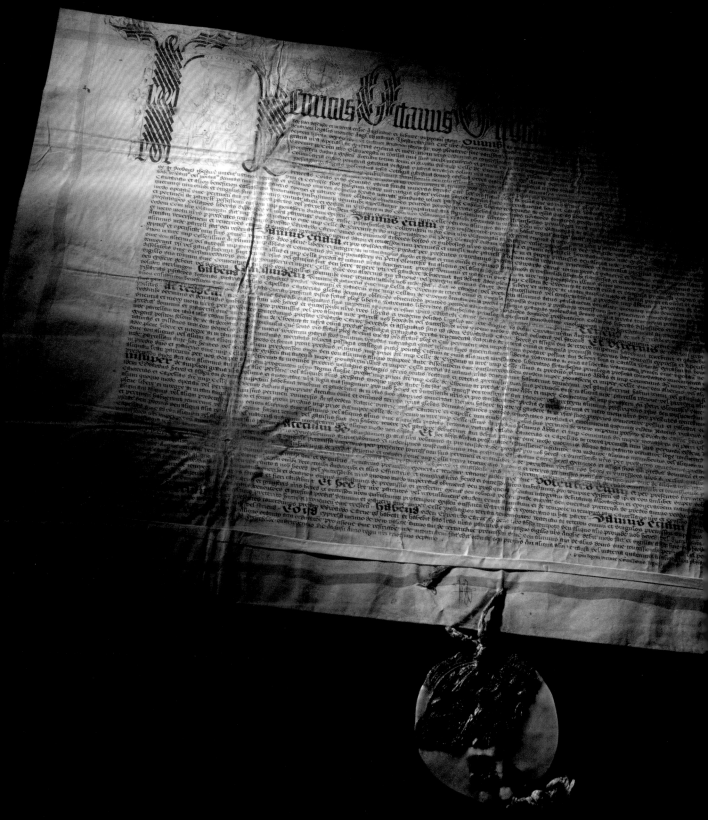

35 Yny lhyvyr hwnn
1546

In 1546, almost a century after Johannes Gutenberg invented moveable type, a printed book was published in the Welsh language for the first time. It has no title and is known by the first words of its contents page, *Yny lhyvyr hwnn* (*In this book*). It is a quarto pamphlet of 32 pages, printed by Edward Whitchurch in London using black letter type. It may not have had a wide circulation – only one copy survives – but its publication marks an important moment in the development of the Welsh language.

The book's compiler was Sir John Prise (or Prys). His early career followed closely that of Edward Carne **[34]**. After training as a lawyer at the University of Oxford he entered the service of Thomas Cromwell. He was a commissioner in the dissolution of the monasteries and benefited personally, acquiring the land and wealth of Hereford and Brecon priories. So successful was his career that the poet Lewys Morgannwg compared it to 'a long summer's day'.

But though he was loyal to the new order Prise had a deep respect for the cultural heritage of the monks. From their libraries he built a collection of over 100 manuscripts, including some from Wales – the Black Book of Carmarthen among them. Prise was a formidable scholar, with a special interest in the origins of Wales and its language. 'Since I was a boy', he wrote, 'I have been versed in the old language of the British and their antiquities.' In the 1540s he began writing *Historiae Britannicae defensio*, a learned defence, drawing in part on Welsh-language sources, of Geoffrey of Monmouth's (mistaken) version of British and Welsh history. He was one of the first Welshmen to belong to a network of Renaissance scholars in England who were in touch with Erasmus and other Continental humanists.

Prise saw clearly that the new technology of print could prove a powerful way of spreading the new Protestant religion, where no intermediate authority stood between the word of God and the people. Since Welsh was the language of most inhabitants of Wales it followed that religious texts needed to be printed in Welsh. In his preface, 'A Welshman sends an address to the readers', Prise says: 'And now that God has placed print in our midst in order to multiply knowledge of his blessed words, it is proper for us, as all Christendom has done, to take a part of this goodness along with them, so that as good a gift as this should be no less fruitful to us than to others.'

But illiteracy remained widespread in Wales. Prise could not take for granted an easy ability to read sacred texts. This is why *Yny lhyvyr hwnn* contains a Welsh alphabet, with a note on spelling and punctuation, and list of numbers, a calendar and almanac, in addition to the Creed, Lord's Prayer, Ave Maria, Ten Commandments and other religious texts. Although the pamphlet was intended as a basic primer, some of its contents, including the parts on the Welsh language, reflected Prise's learning, derived from reading the manuscripts he had collected.

Yny lhyvyr hwnn was the first of 108 books published in Welsh between 1546 and 1660. Though not large, this total compares well with publishing in the other minority languages of Europe. Slowly, Welsh was becoming established as a language of the printed word.

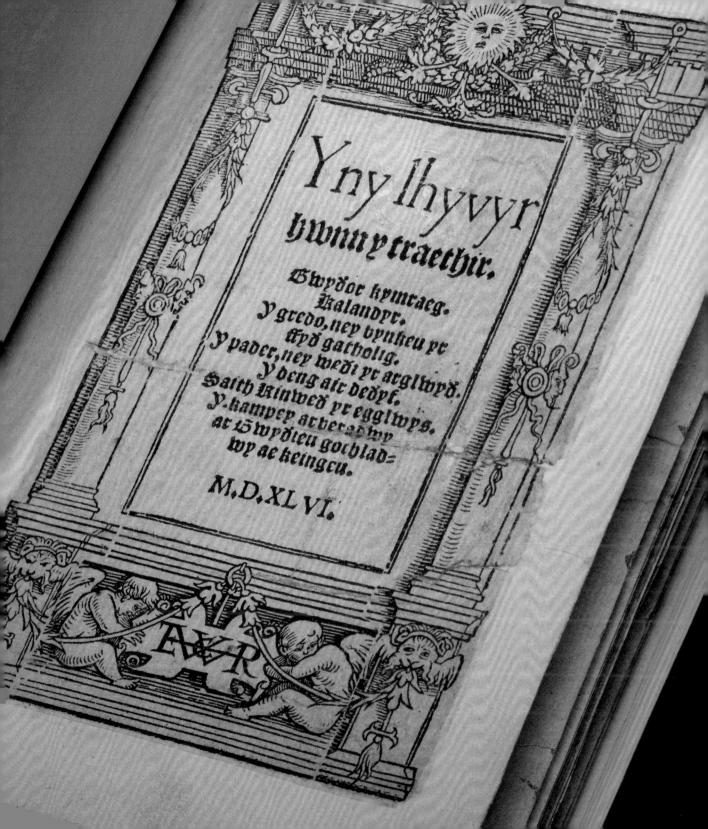

Yny lhyvyr hwnn y traethir.

Gwydor kymraeg.
Kalandyr.
Y gredo, ney bynkeu yr
ffyd gatholig.
Y pader, ney wedi yr arglwyd.
Y deng air dedyf.
Saith rinwed yr eglwys.
Y kampeu at weras wy
ar Gwydieu gochlad=
wy ac keingeu.

M.D.XL VI.

A V R

36 Humphrey Llwyd's map of Wales
1573

Maps tell us where we are. But they also tell us, and others, who we are. Humphrey Llwyd, the author of the first published map of Wales as a distinct country, was determined that the wider world should be aware of Wales and its history and geography.

Llwyd was born in Denbigh in 1527 and graduated at the University of Oxford. He served the Earl of Arundel, developing an interest in humanist scholarship and building a large library. In 1563 he returned to his home town and spent the rest of his life researching and publishing, mainly in Welsh history.

A chance meeting in Antwerp in 1567 with another Denbigh man, Richard Clough, led to Llwyd's introduction to the pioneering mapmaker Abraham Ortelius. Llwyd promised to supply two maps to Ortelius, one of Wales and the other of England and Wales, to be included in his great work *Theatrum orbis terrarum*, one of the first printed world atlases. Already ill, Llwyd wrote to Ortelius in August 1568, 'I send unto you my Wales, not beautifully set forth in all poynctes, yet truly depeinted, so be that certeyn notes be observed, which I gathered even when I was ready to die'. 'Wales' was published in a supplement to the *Theatrum* in 1573 under the title 'Cambriae Typus', along with Llwyd's notes. It was influential and was reprinted fifty times between 1573 and 1741.

'Cambriae Typus' was a by-product of Llwyd's historical and topographical research. His first gift to Ortelius, printed in the *Theatrum* in 1570, was an essay on the name and antiquities of Anglesey, 'Mona, island of the Druids' **[49]**. His map, measuring 456mm by 348mm, was not the result of original surveying. Llwyd relied on earlier maps, including a version of Mercator's

map of 1564, corrected according to information available to him. This explains the many inaccuracies, which increase the further Llwyd moves from his native north-east Wales. Llŷn sags to the south; St Brides Bay, the Gower peninsula and Swansea Bay are absent; the Glamorgan coastline is rounded; and 'Myrthyr Tydfal' and Worm's Head are misplaced.

The boundaries of Wales extend into the English border counties, since the patriotic Llwyd wished to show not contemporary but ancient Wales, separated by the rivers Dee and Severn from 'Lhoëgria, or if you prefer, England'. He lists the Welsh, English and 'British' forms of place names, and includes supplementary information. Aberffraw was 'once the royal palace of all Wales'; Denbigh is 'the author's birthplace'; Bangor-on-Dee had 'a monastery with 2,200 monks'; Montgomery, 'once known for its excellent horses, now produces few'; the river Teifi is 'the only river in Britain with beavers'. South Pembrokeshire is where the Flemings were settled, 'different from the Welsh in their language and customs'.

Llwyd did not live to see his map in print. He died in 1568 and was buried in St Marcella's church, Llanfarchell (Eglwys Wen or Whitchurch). An elaborate tomb there shows him kneeling in prayer; at the apex of the pediment is an orb, symbolising his geographical expertise.

When Christopher Saxton compiled his more detailed, but unpublished, map of Wales in 1580, he used surveying techniques to correct Llwyd's errors. Saxton was a Yorkshireman and used English rather than Welsh place names. This tradition continued into the Ordnance Survey era. Only recently have maps been published showing the Welsh forms of place names.

CAMBRI
AE TYPVS
Auctore
HVMFRE
DO LHV,
YDO
Denbigiense Cam-
brobritano

HI,
BER,
NIAE
PARS.

Dublin

SEPTENTRIO

Mona insula. L.
Anglesey. A.
Mon. B.

VERGIVIVM SIVE HIBERNICVM MARE
MOR WERIDH, Britannis,
THE YRISHE OCEANE, Anglis.

L. A. B. literæ, vocabulis
aliquando notant illud esse
Latinum, Anglicum, aut
Britannicum, quod est
incolarum.

Scala Milia
Anglicorum.

20

40

60

37 Portrait of Sir John Perrot
Undated

This undated oil painting by an anonymous artist is probably based on an earlier portrait. Its jovial, jaunty image hardly conveys the character of the man it portrays: 'a man in stature very tall and big ... his countenance full of majestie, his eye marvellous percing, and carrying a commaunding aspect, insomuch that when he was angrie, he had a terrible visage or looke ... He was by nature very cholericke and could not brooke any crosses.'

This, in the words of his son, is Sir John Perrot (1528-1592), a Pembrokeshire chancer, adventurer and plutocrat. He led a rackety and violent life, serving a succession of monarchs and enriching himself in the process.

Perrot was brought up by his stepfather, Sir Henry Jones, in Haroldston, Haverfordwest [24] and educated at the cathedral school in St Davids. Aged eighteen he was sent to serve William Paulet, later Marquess of Winchester, and through him gained access to the royal court. Skilful use of his connections then secured him a rapid succession of honours: he became MP for Carmarthenshire in 1547, a knight in 1549 and sheriff of Pembrokeshire in 1552. By now Perrot had integrated himself fully into the English ruling class. After a difficult period during the reign of Mary Tudor he returned to favour with Elizabeth I and gained so many offices and so much land in Pembrokeshire that he was virtual ruler of the county. His acquisitiveness and frequent resort to law provoked fierce local opposition. Perrot made enemies easily.

Then he accepted a new office, the first President of Munster. In 1571 he arrived in Ireland to suppress a rebellion led by James Fitzmaurice Fitzgerald.

His methods were brutal – over 800 rebels were executed by hanging – but ineffective, and he resigned from the post in 1573, returning home to Pembrokeshire and vowing 'to lead a countryman's life and to keep out of debt'. He had inherited Carew Castle [33] and began a building programme there to create a sumptuous home for himself, paid for in part from the extortionate rents he charged his tenants. He did the same with the castle at Laugharne in Carmarthenshire, granted to him by the Queen in 1575. These works remained unfinished; Perrot's retirement was short-lived.

In 1584 he was sent back to Ireland as Lord Deputy. His task was to subjugate the Irish and begin the process of colonisation. Again his strong-arm tactics and lack of diplomacy led to mixed success and he asked permission to leave. After nine years he had alienated many of his colleagues, and although he was given one further post, planning the defence of south-west Wales against Spanish invasion, his enemies were determined to overthrow him. On flimsy evidence they accused him of treason and conspiring with the king of Spain to remove the Queen. In 1592 he was tried, found guilty and condemned to death. He died in the Tower of London, possibly by poisoning, before he could be executed.

Perrot was typical of Tudor Welshmen who gathered wealth and power by assimilating themselves into the English élite. He was one of the first Welshmen to play a leading part in English colonial oppression and imperial expansion. A contemporary portrait of him, a rough stone head now in Carmarthen Museum, conveys better than the painting the asperity that role demanded.

38 William Morgan's Bible
1588

It was not inevitable that a Bible would be published in the Welsh language during the sixteenth century. The 1536 Act of Union had banned the use of Welsh in official life, and English was increasingly the language of Welsh gentry.

But the logic of Protestantism, with its emphasis on the primacy of the word of God, pointed towards making scripture directly accessible to the people in their own language – even if that language was Welsh **[35]**. Government-sanctioned English Bibles were published from 1538, and in 1563 an Act of Parliament licensed the publication of a Bible and Prayer Book in Welsh. A New Testament was published in 1567. William Salesbury's pioneering translation, though scholarly, used a perverse system of spelling and was given a cool reception. About ten years later a cleric and scholar of rare ability, William Morgan, took up the challenge of producing a more readable translation, this time of the whole Bible, including the Apocrypha.

Morgan was born into a modestly endowed family of tenant farmers at Tŷ Mawr, Wybrnant, near Penmachno. He was taken up by the cultured landowner Sir John Wynn of Gwydir, and eventually entered the University of Cambridge. He stayed there for thirteen years, gaining four degrees and a thorough knowledge of Latin, Greek and Hebrew, ideal skills for a Biblical scholar. He may have begun his translation before he moved to Llanrhaeadr-ym-Mochnant as vicar in 1578.

It is likely that Morgan already had a backer prepared to pay for the printing, possibly John Whitgift, Archbishop of Canterbury. Their aim may have been to speed the decline of Catholicism, and also to avert a threat from extreme Protestants. In his Latin preface Morgan defended his translation by arguing that the urgency of the religious need made the use of Welsh essential.

Most Bible translations were, and are, produced by teams, but Morgan worked largely alone, from the Hebrew and Greek of the original texts and with the help of Salesbury's New Testament, English translations and many commentaries. His version had many virtues. It was accurate. It used a form of Welsh that, though elevated from ordinary speech, was easily understood. Spellings were natural and standardised. Above all, Morgan's Welsh style, building on a rich heritage of earlier prose and poetry, was strong and memorable. 'There is no portrait of him', says the poet R.S. Thomas, but his 'rows of teeth / broken on the unmanageable bone / of language' produced 'passages of serene prose'.

In 1587 Morgan brought his completed manuscript to London to oversee its printing. Composing, printing and proof-reading took a whole year. On 22 September 1588 the Bible, 1,116 pages long and printed by the 'Deputies of Christopher Barker, printer to the Queen', was ready. Copies were ordered to be sent, priced at £1 each, to every church in Wales.

The religious and linguistic influence of Morgan's work was profound. After 1588 people could hear the words of the Bible in their own language every week. The poet Siôn Mawddwy wrote, 'Famous lord, you led us blind people out of darkness'. Morgan's literary Welsh set a pattern for generations to follow, though at first, even for the literate, it was transmitted orally rather than on paper. Individual readers could not buy a Little Bible, sold at a crown, until 1630, and personal copies were uncommon until the eighteenth century.

Y BEIBL CYS-SEGR-LAN. SEF YR HEN DESTA-MENT, A'R NEWYDD.

2. Timoth. 3. 14, 15.

Eithr aros di yn y pethau a ddyscaist, ac a ymddyried-
wydi ti, gan wybod gan bwy y dyscaist.
Ac i ti eryn fachgen wybod yr scrythur lân, yr hon
sydd abl i'th wneuthur yn ddoeth i iechydwria-
eth, trwy'r ffydd yr hon sydd yng-Hrist Iesu.

Imprinted at London by the Deputies of
CHRISTOPHER BARKER,
Printer to the Queenes most excel-
lent Maiestie.

1588.

39 John Davies's Welsh grammar
1621

At the same time as Welsh became established as a language of the Bible, it began to be studied for the first time by scholars as a language in its own right. They compiled Welsh dictionaries and grammars to show how the language had evolved and how it worked in practice. The first Welsh-English dictionary was published by William Salesbury [38] in 1547, and Gruffydd Robert began to publish the first Welsh grammar in Milan in 1567. But it was John Davies of Mallwyd, acknowledged as the greatest of Wales's Renaissance scholars – 'the excellent, the one and only Plato of our language', as one contemporary described him – who brought new, rigorous standards to the emerging study of the Welsh language.

John Davies was the son of a Denbighshire weaver. After a grammar school education, perhaps in Ruthin, he studied at Jesus College, Oxford and worked for William Morgan in Llandaff and St Asaph. In 1604, probably with Morgan's support, he became rector of Mallwyd in Merioneth and remained there for forty years. Here he wrote, in an astonishingly fertile period, a series of influential works. He was mainly responsible for the revision of Morgan's translation of the Bible published in 1620. A year later he published a revised Welsh translation of the Book of Common Prayer. Also in 1621 appeared his Welsh grammar, *Antiquae linguae Britannicae rudimenta*. This was followed in 1632 by a dictionary, *Antiquae linguae Britannicae dictionarium duplex*. He wrote the Welsh-Latin section of the dictionary himself, and revised a Latin-Welsh section written by Thomas Wiliems.

Underlying all Davies's scholarship was a deep understanding of earlier writing in Welsh. He sought out manuscripts of early poetry, like the Hendregadredd Manuscript, and copied out their contents. In his grammar, written in Latin for international scholars to read, he gives a masterly analysis of the Welsh language. He tries to establish its antiquity by claiming that 'the British language has a close affinity with the oriental languages', especially Hebrew.

Davies was an intellectual, but he was also a man of the world. In a witty reference to the exiled Roman poet Ovid he once joked of Mallwyd that it was like Scythia, a cultural desert. But he cared enough about the village to create his own architectural designs to rebuild the rectory and the church, and to build several bridges.

In the eighteenth century this copy of Davies's grammar was owned by Richard Morris, one of Morrisiaid Môn [47], and then by the Anglesey poet and writer Goronwy Owen. As a writer, Owen's aim was to use Welsh poetic forms to emulate the new classical verse of English poets like Pope and Dryden. Opposite the title page Goronwy inscribed this *englyn* in Latin, in praise of John Davies's grammar and, by extension, the Welsh language. Goronwy signs the poem as 'Grono Owain'. He was just sixteen years old when he wrote it in 1738.

Devia usque ad Davis – veluti
Vallata tenebris,
Nunc age, salvaque sis,
Ianua Cambrigenis

Lost till the age of Davies,
Walled in by darkness,
Now come alive and prosper,
A gate for the Welsh people.

(54.)

ANTIQVÆ
LINGVÆ BRITANNICÆ,
nunc communiter dictæ
CAMBRO-BRITANNICÆ,
à suis
CYMRAECAE vel CAMBRICAE,
ab aliis
WALLICÆ,
RVDIMENTA:

Iuxtà genuinam naturalemq́; ipsius
linguæ proprietatem,

Quâ fieri potuit accurata methodo &
brevitate conscripta.

LONDINI,
Apud IOHANNEM BILLIVM,
Typographum Regium.
1621.

40 Estate map of Barry
1622

Land in Wales, until at least the industrial revolution, meant power. Owning land, especially if it was fertile, brought income from crops, rents and tolls, as well as political influence and social status. After Oliver St John succeeded his father as 4th Baron St John of Bletso in 1618, he employed a surveyor called Evans Mouse to make a detailed map and terrier or inventory of his estates, including those in the Vale of Glamorgan centred on Fonmon Castle. Mapping not only confirmed to St John what he owned, it helped to manage his tenants and protect him against litigation by other landlords.

Fonmon Castle had been in the hands of the St John family and their predecessors since about 1200. By the 1600s its land included the manors of Fonmon, Llancadle, Penmark and Barry. Like other Glamorgan gentry Oliver St John was an absentee landlord. His Fonmon estates were managed and leased out to his brother, Sir Anthony St John, to whom Mouse dedicated his maps.

Little is known about Evans Mouse. He was presumably a Welshman and was certainly a highly professional surveyor. His maps, produced in 1622, are among the earliest and best manorial maps to survive in Wales. Drawn in ink and watercolour on thick parchment to a scale of about 50cm to a mile, they are accurate and meticulously detailed. No better map of the area was produced before the Ordnance Survey began its mapping over 200 years later.

The maps show rivers (coloured turquoise), roads and lanes (brown), buildings (red roofs) and field boundaries. Fields (in green) are numbered and the terrier gives individual field names and acreages.

By 1622 the process of enclosing common land was now all but complete: just a few of the former communally-tilled strip fields are visible on the Barry sheet. The fourteen tenant farmers were copyholders, their rights and duties established by custom. As well as paying rent to the landlord, they were expected to give their best cow (or 6 shillings) to the lord each year, and could only grind corn at the lord's mill. 'Barreye Castle ruinated' is marked on the map, along with St Nicholas's church and 'Cold Knappe, invironed with the sea of all partes' and separated from the mainland by a salt marsh.

The shape of pre-industrial Barry had become established by 1622. Ownership patterns, however, changed over time. A land survey of about 1812 shows that the number of tenants had reduced from fourteen to four, as larger farms proved more economic. Even large landlords were not exempt from change. Oliver St John, the 5th Baron Bletso and son of the maps' commissioner, found himself in financial difficulties during the period of the Commonwealth and sold Fonmon Castle and three of the manors in 1658. The buyer was a leading Parliamentarian, Philip Jones of Llangyfelach. He was governor of Swansea in 1645, took part in the Battle of St Fagans in 1648 and became a trusted aide of Oliver Cromwell when war ceased. He succeeded in keeping his estates after the Restoration in 1660, and built extensions to Fonmon Castle.

In 1881 Barry was still rural, with a population of about 500. Once David Davies of Llandinam [69] decided to build his new coal-exporting docks, first opened in 1889, its population increased dramatically, reaching 38,945 in 1921.

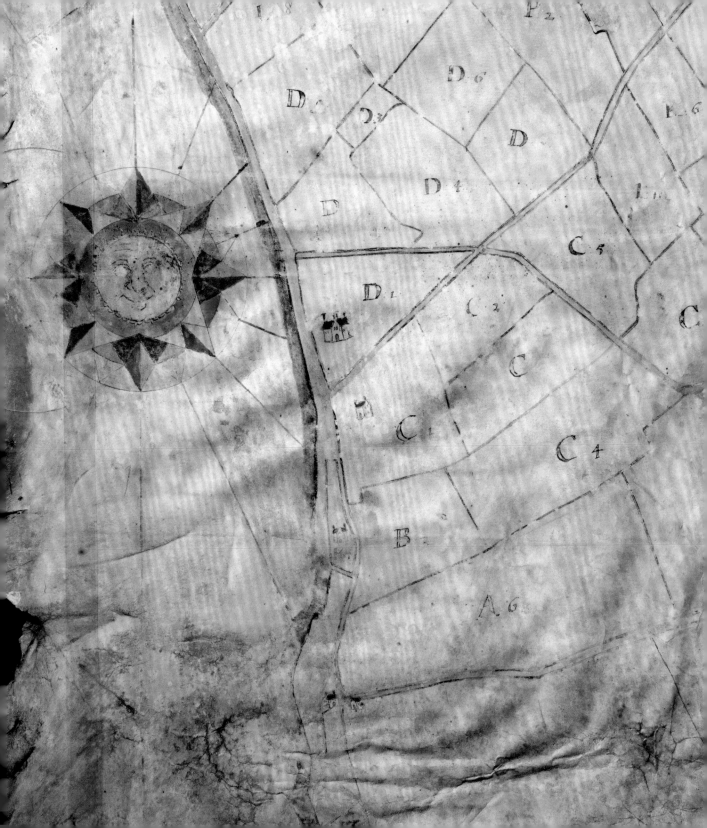

4·1 Silver coins from the Aberystwyth Mint
1639-42

Metals – iron, copper, gold, lead and silver – were mined in Wales in Roman times and before **[4, 10]**. By the late sixteenth century entrepreneurs were digging into the hills of mid-Wales in search of silver to be made into coins and other objects. In 1625 Sir Hugh Myddelton of Denbigh won a royal licence – gold or silver mines belonged by law to the Crown – to extract silver in Cardiganshire. His widow sold the lease in 1636 to an English speculator of dubious methods, Thomas Bushell. Bushell had worked for Francis Bacon, the philosopher, scientist and Lord Chancellor, and from him, it seems, he learned the skills of mining engineering.

In 1637 Bushell wrote to Charles I asking permission to set up a royal mint in Aberystwyth, arguing that transporting his silver to the mint in London was dangerous and costly. Despite objections from the London Mint, the King agreed: from 1629 to 1640 he ruled without a parliament and was always anxious to increase his income. And so, from January 1639 until September 1642, Bushell mined silver in Cwmsymlog; in his mint in Aberystwyth Castle, as 'warden and master worker', he produced coins for the King worth a total of £10,500.

Bushell issued coins in a wide variety of denomination: half crown, shilling, sixpence, groat (4d), threepence, twopence, penny and halfpenny. Some of them feature two special devices: the Prince of Wales feathers show the Welsh origin of the coins, and an open book seems to have been Bushell's privy mark or shorthand for 'made in Aberystwyth'.

By now relations between King and Parliament had broken down, and in August 1642 the Civil War began. Thomas Bushell fled Aberystwyth almost immediately.

Still a convinced Royalist, he ended the war on Lundy Island, defending the last part of Britain to surrender to the victorious Parliamentary armies. The mint was moved, first to Shrewsbury, Charles's new base, and then to Oxford and Bristol, though it seems to have made a brief reappearance in 1648 in the village of Furnace, north of Aberystwyth.

In Wales there was comparatively little enthusiasm for the Parliamentary cause. Most preferred to keep out of the fray, if they could, rather than commit to the King's cause. Nevertheless, the country became a battlefield for the opposing forces. The Parliamentary armies, led by Rowland Laugharne, and the Royalists, led by Charles Gerard, fought for dominance in south Wales. Aberystwyth Castle was badly damaged in 1646 and razed in 1649. A brief peace came with the defeat of the King in 1647, but the renewed Civil War raged across Wales, culminating in Oliver Cromwell's victory in the Battle of St Fagans in May 1648.

Over the next two centuries mining for lead intensified in north Cardiganshire. Lewis Morris, the writer and scholar from Anglesey **[47]**, was appointed superintendent of the King's mines, though he soon fell out with the local gentry. By the mid-nineteenth century a large workforce was employed, often in squalid and hazardous conditions, in mines dominated by owners from Derbyshire and Cornwall **[57]**.

Coin-making returned to Wales in 1968 with the opening of the Royal Mint in Llantrisant. This was one result of the Labour government's policy, begun with the establishing of the Welsh Office in 1964, of devolving central administrative functions out of London – a late echo of Charles I's decision of 1637.

4·2 John Ogilby's road maps
1675

Until the late eighteenth century travelling any distance on land within Wales was difficult, slow and sometimes dangerous. The Romans' network of well-made roads had not been renewed. In 1188 it took Giraldus Cambrensis **[17, 19]** six weeks to travel 500 miles around Wales; a traveller could not have made the same journey in 1500 very much faster.

As population, administration and trade increased, roads began to grow in importance, though governments rarely recognised any responsibility for their building or upkeep. Drovers **[53]**, taking cattle from upland Wales to markets in England from the fifteenth century onward, developed long-distance routes, though they were often little more than muddy tracks. In 1555 an Act of Parliament obliged parishes to appoint two persons as 'surveyors of highways', and all able-bodied men in the parish were to donate four days each year to road repair. It had little effect. A road-mending day was known as a *diwrnod i'r brenin* or 'a day for the king' – a euphemism for idling and relaxation.

In 1675 a Scot, John Ogilby, published a guide for travellers that showed how to negotiate the roads of England and Wales between distant points. His unconventional atlas, entitled *Britannia*, included a series of one hundred strip maps, each following selected roads between two points and noting the immediately adjacent terrain and places through which they passed.

John Ogilby was a man of ingenuity and enterprise. At various times he was a tutor and dance teacher, translator, theatre impresario and publisher, before his appointment in 1671 by Charles II as 'His Majesty's Cosmographer and Geographic Printer'. He included 7,700 miles of road in the 85 routes he selected for publication in *Britannia*. To improve accuracy in surveying he used a dimensurator or measuring wheel, rather than a surveyor's chain, and he adopted a scale of one inch to one mile (the mile of 1,760 yards was standardised for the first time).

Plate 67 of the atlas is the second of two plates showing the route from St Davids to Holywell – an unlikely route, perhaps. Beginning in Tal-y-bont, Ceredigion, it heads north to Machynlleth, follows the river Dovey to Mallwyd, crosses the mountains to Bala, and passes through Ruthin to Holywell. Colours were added by hand after printing. Ogilby marks rivers (blue), lakes (green), bridges, gates and junctions. Hills (brown) have their up and down slopes indicated separately. Ogilby shows orientation though yellow compasses, which differ from strip to strip, and includes distances, very accurately for the period.

Ogilby's innovative maps were popular. They were reprinted and pirated, and published from 1719 in more portable editions. The roads of Wales, though, stayed unimproved until the period between 1750 and 1850, when Parliament licensed turnpike trusts to improve the quality of the major routes with the use of tolls. In Wales the imposition of tolls proved a flashpoint for dissatisfaction felt by already impoverished rural workers. Between 1839 and 1843 'Rebecca and her daughters', men wearing women's clothes, attacked tollgates and threatened their keepers with violence in a campaign across south-west Wales. Military force was needed to suppress the uprising. But the protestors were vindicated. From 1844 county-based roads boards replaced the ineffective turnpike companies, and the roads of Wales finally began to improve.

4·3 Cwpwrdd tridarn
Late 17th century

The cwpwrdd tridarn or three-part cupboard was unique to Snowdonia and its surrounding area. It was a common sight in the houses of wealthier farmers and gentry. While newer styles began to influence furniture elsewhere, the local tradition survived and flourished, from around 1660 to about 1770.

Cypyrddau tridarn were made by skilled local carpenters from seasoned oak. The middle and lower parts were true cupboards for storing clothes and other goods. The top section, below a canopy supported by turned columns, was left open to display pottery, pewter and other family treasures. Some *cypyrddau* were elaborately carved with mouldings, inlaid panels, figures and inscriptions, while others, like the example from Ynysgain Fawr near Cricieth, were much plainer.

A family might commission a *cwpwrdd tridarn* to mark an important event, like a marriage or setting up a new home. A *cwpwrdd* of 1689 now in Tŷ Mawr, Wybrnant [38] records the initials of a couple, 'WI' and 'IH', followed by a motto, '*Bydd drugarog yn ôl dy allu*' ('Have mercy in accordance with your power'). The *cwpwrdd tridarn* was a practical as well as an impressive piece of furniture, since it occupied little floor space in what were usually far from large houses.

The house at Ynysgain was replaced by a new one in the late eighteenth century, but the Jones (later Pughe-Jones) family, who lived there continuously from the mid-seventeenth century until 1955, passed their *cwpwrdd tridarn* proudly from one generation to the next. Pride in a rural craft tradition and its survival is a theme of D.J. Williams's elegiac short story '*Y cwpwrdd tridarn*', written in 1939. Its central character, an old stonemason called Harri Bach, comes to the painful realisation that his nephew, John Hendri, has rejected traditional Welsh culture and language. Harri's only remaining possession, to be left to John after his death, is his ancestral *cwpwrdd*, where he keeps his few remaining treasures. 'Unknown to him, it acted as an anchor in the deep, protecting his nature from the sea's constant ebb and flow around him'. Now, he notices, woodworm infests it.

Ynysgain was the home of one of the earliest black Africans recorded in Wales. His birth date and name are unknown, and how he came to the Criccieth area as a boy around 1745 is uncertain. One story, according to an account transmitted orally and published by 'Alltud Eifion' in 1888, was that he was captured in Africa by a member of the Wynne family of Ystumllyn, but he may have come from a slave household in the West Indies. When he arrived at Ystumllyn he was said to have had 'no language other than sounds similar to the howling of a dog', but he soon became fluent in Welsh and English. Local people knew him as John Ystumllyn or Jack Black. A skilled horticulturalist and florist, he worked as a gardener for the Wynne family.

An oil painting shows John as a handsome youth, and he was said to be attractive to local girls. He first came to Ynysgain when courting Margaret Gruffydd. After marrying they lived at Ynysgain, working there as land stewards. John died in 1786 and was buried at Ynyscynhaearn. His memorial stone there includes an *englyn* by Dafydd Siôn Siâms, evidence that he was, as tradition reports, 'respected by the gentry and the common people alike' as an honest and principled man.

4.4. Jacobite glasses
c.1740-1775

The richest man in Wales in the first half of the eighteenth century was Sir Watkin Williams Wynn of Wynnstay, 3rd baronet. By 1720, through inheritance and marriage, he had amassed an estate of over 100,000 acres across five Welsh counties.

Wynn was an avid and reactionary politician, with firm views against the Whigs. Political success demanded lavish expenditure. He spent a fortune on creating and bribing electors to vote himself and others into Parliament – he was an MP almost continuously from 1716 to his death in 1749. He did not disguise his sympathy with the exiled Stuarts, who attempted to regain the throne by force in 1715 and 1745. In 1715 he may have incited anti-Hanoverian riots in Wrexham; in 1722 he burned a picture of George I in public, and he promised his support to Charles Edward Stuart, if Charles invaded with a French army. The French failed to appear, allowing Wynn to avoid commitment to Charles and, when the rebellion failed, punishment by the government.

Wynn was not the only Stuart sympathiser. On 10 June 1710, the birthday of James Stuart, the Old Pretender, he organised fellow-Jacobites in north-east Wales into a society, the Cycle Club (meetings cycled between members' houses in and around Wrexham) The Cycle was neither wholly secret nor entirely serious in its sedition. After the failure of 1745 it was little more than a nostalgic dining and drinking club. The members drank their wine, however, from the very best glasses, made especially for them by English glassmakers and often engraved with Jacobite messages.

Wynn's estates and fortune were inherited by the 4th baronet, also called Sir Watkin Williams Wynn. His interests lay in art, music and drama. To celebrate coming of age he held a party at Wynnstay for 15,000 guests; it was reported that 'three coaches full of cooks were sent from London'. He commissioned an architect, James Byers, to design a new palace to replace his existing house. Byers's surviving drawings show what an extravagant cultural centre, including a large concert hall with grand staircase, would have graced the banks of the Dee if they had been realised. Instead, Wynn built a new town house in London, dividing his time between London and Wales.

Wynn was a keen promoter of Welsh culture. In London he supported a Welsh charity school and two early Welsh societies, the Society of Antient Britons and the Honourable Society of Cymmrodorion. At Wynnstay he helped Richard Wilson and Paul Sandby, two of the earliest landscape artists of Wales, and the harpist John Parry.

The power and patronage of the Wynns were long remembered. A song collected in the nineteenth century claimed that Wynn was 'a king in the hearts of his tenants everywhere'. In 1996 Bob Delyn a'r Ebillion sang more satirically of the son and his wife: in translation, 'Our smart friends say (no caveats), / The two of us are the hippest of cats / With our chandeliers and costly hats / And Mo-o-o-o-o-ozart.'

Drawing for Wynnstay concert hall by James Byers (National Library of Wales)

4.5 Map of Howell Harris's travels

1740s

On 25 May 1735 a young man went to communion in Talgarth church and had a strange experience. Suddenly he was 'convinced by the Holy Ghost, that Christ dyed for me, and that all my sins were laid on him', and he was engulfed by a state of 'peace, joy, watchfulness, hatred to sin, and fear of offending God'.

This moment was part of a personal conversion for Howell Harris. It was also, by tradition, the beginning of a new movement of enthusiasm and personal salvation within the established Church, which would eventually lead to a new and powerful independent establishment, the Presbyterian Church of Wales.

The son of a carpenter, Harris was born in Trefeca near Talgarth in 1714. His autobiography paints a lurid and probably exaggerated picture of his youth, when he was 'carried away with the stream of vanity, pride, and youthful diversions' and 'atheistical thoughts', so that 'all my corruptions grew stronger and stronger in me'. Harris was far from being the first 'enthusiast'. One of his mentors, Griffith Jones of Llanddowror, also a religious convert, toured parishes urging that souls should be saved – though he is best known for the elementary schools he established to spread basic literacy among adults and children in south-west Wales. Nor was Harris alone: another charismatic preacher was Daniel Rowland, whose ecstatic followers were known as 'jumpers'. 'Enthusiasm' arose from a combination of factors: an inactive Church of England, the rise of an increasingly literate people open to new ideas, and the influence of similar religious movements in England and beyond.

On his conversion day, Harris wrote, 'I felt some insatiable desires after the salvation of poor sinners;

my heart longed for their being convinced of their sins and misery.' In 1736 he took to the road to spread his message: at first locally, then throughout Wales and parts of England. He often encountered hostility from clergy, gentry and others. 'The gentlemen', he wrote, 'hunt us like partridges'. But he attracted large audiences and gained many followers. He organised them into 'societies', whose members gave one another religious support and discipline. In 1748 Harris wrote: 'I have now visited [in nine weeks] 13 Counties & travaild mostly 150 Miles every week, & Discoursed twice every Day, & sometimes three & four times a Day; & this last Journey I have not taken off my Cloaths for 7 Nights.' All the while he wrote a detailed diary in 284 volumes, and thousands of letters. On a handwritten map of his travels Harris lists some of his destinations: Lampeter and Llangeitho, St Davids and Haverfordwest, Shrewsbury, Birmingham, and London.

After ten years of toil Harris was worn out: 'he frequently neglected his health, and was indifferent to food … and even to sleep'. He was a difficult man, arrogant, obsessive and humourless. 'I had a temptation to laugh last night', he wrote in his diary, fearing an onset of hysteria. He quarrelled with Daniel Rowland and others over doctrine, was criticised for a close relationship with a married woman, and finally retreated to Trefeca in 1752. There he set up a religious commune. 'The Family', as he called it, numbered 29 people by 1753 and 120 ten years later. In time Trefeca had a chapel, a bakery, gardens, an infirmary and even a printing press.

4·6 Crwth y Foelas
1742

One moonlit night the Black Crwth Player was walking home when he was surrounded by a hungry pack of wolves. To deter them he started to play his crwth, but soon they prepared to attack him. He redoubled his efforts and played without a break all through the night. The wolves listened, entranced. When men approached they vanished and the musician went on his way.

This legend preserves a memory of the potency of an ancient stringed instrument. The crwth was once common throughout Europe, but it held a special place, along with the harp, in music-making in medieval Welsh courts. It is mentioned in the *trioedd cerdd* (musical/ poetic triads), where it is associated with *cerdd dant*, the traditional singing of lyrics to instrumental accompaniment. It could be played with three strings, but six strings were more common. In a lavish festival held by Rhys ap Gruffydd in Cardigan Castle at Christmas 1176 crwth players played in competition with harpists and pipers. After 1600 the crwth was adopted for use in popular music. But by the end of the eighteenth century it had been displaced by the fiddle. The antiquary Daines Barrington wrote in 1770, 'The chief reason of my having sent this ancient instrument called a crwth to the Society [of Antiquaries] for their inspection is, that it is now perhaps on the very point of being entirely lost, as there is but one person in the whole principality who can now play upon it. His name is John Morgan of Newburgh, in the island of Anglesey, who is now fifty-nine years of age; so that the instrument will probably die with him in a few years'.

Very few original crwths survive today. Crwth y Foelas is the best preserved. Inscribed '1742', it was made by Richard Evans of Llanfihangel Bachellaeth, near Pwllheli. Its simple box soundboard, with its two circular sound-holes, is attached to a central fretless neck or fingerboard, fixed in place by a U-shaped yoke. The bridge is flat, so that it is easy for a bow to play all the strings at once. There are six gut strings. Two of them are placed away from the line of the fingerboard and can be used as a drone or plucked with the thumb. Despite some lists of crwth tunes like 'Dugan y Crythor Du' ('Air of the Black Crwth Player'), and some information from early nineteenth century musicians like Edward Jones, 'Bardd y Brenin', it is hard to know now exactly how the crwth was tuned or played, and or what music was played on it. One poet likened its sound to 'a hundred voices in one hand'. It had a range of an octave and a half. A replica of a crwth played today has a drone-like quality, but in skilled hands it is capable of a surprising range of harmonies.

X-rays of Crwth y Foelas and two of the other original crwths revealed that a tapering cavity runs inside the whole length of the fingerboard – possibly to create a second, supplementary soundboard to amplify the instrument.

The crwth received new attention during the revival of the Welsh folk music tradition in the 1980s. Replica instruments were built, and some musicians, notably Cass Meurig and Robert Evans, have performed and recorded music for the crwth.

4.7 Lewis Morris's chart of Caernarvon bar and harbour

1748

Eighteenth century roads in Wales were poor and slow. Often the easiest way to transport goods and people was by sea. A stream of barques, barges, brigantines, brigs, cruisers, cutters, packets, sloops, smacks and other vessels sailed from harbour to harbour along the coast, and to major ports like Liverpool, Bristol and Dublin. But the sea was hazardous. Dozens of Welsh vessels were lost in the Great Storm of 1703. The lack of reliable charts made coastal voyages even more dangerous.

Lewis Morris was determined to improve matters. He was one of four brothers known as Morrisiaid Môn (the Morrises of Anglesey). Born in 1701, he was brought up at Pentre Eirianell near the east coast of the island. His parents were steeped in Welsh literature and music but far from wealthy, and Lewis, a boy of great intelligence and versatility, was mainly self-taught. For five years he worked as a land surveyor for Owen Meyrick of Bodorgan, before being appointed as a customs officer at Holyhead and Beaumaris. Maps and shipping came together in an ambitious plan he devised to create accurate charts of the coastline of Wales.

In 1736 Morris approached the Admiralty in London with his proposal. It was rejected, but he persevered and finally, in 1737, he was given five shillings a day and release from his customs duties to begin his survey. He started at Beaumaris on 4 July, hiring his own boat, and within a month he had completed surveying the Anglesey coast. In April 1738 he sent eleven large manuscript charts of the coast to the Admiralty. Again he met with rejection; the Customs authorities refused to give him further leave to continue the work. In 1742, through Meyrick's

intervention, the Admiralty was persuaded to allow Morris to resume. Now with a suitable boat, he was able to take soundings and complete his hydrographical survey as far as Tenby. Finally, in 1748, with the Admiralty's permission, he succeeded in publishing his charts through private subscription.

Plans of harbours, bars, bays and roads in St George's Channel consisted of 25 plans covering the Welsh coast from Conwy to Tenby (Morris also published a one-sheet summary of the coast). In his preface he explains the genesis of his work: 'the melancholy Accounts of Shipwrecks, and Losses, so frequent on the Coast of Wales', caused by the 'very slender Knowledge' of its geography. His charts were accurate and clearly drawn. Place names are marked 'according to their true Orthography' rather than the approximate spellings of previous cartographers unfamiliar with Wales. The book was a success and 2,000 copies were sold. Morris's son William later completed the survey and in 1800-1 published his new charts, along with revised versions of his father's.

Lewis Morris had a restless, curious mind. He combined a devotion to Welsh-language culture with a thirst for knowledge of all kinds characteristic of the Age of Enlightenment. 'The printing press', he wrote in 1735, 'is the candle of the world, and the freedom of the Children of Britain [the Welsh]. Why should not we (who were once long ago brave people, if we can be believed) seek some of this light?' As well as surveying, Morris wrote poetry, published on philology, history and music, opened lead mines [41], farmed, began a printing press, copied Welsh manuscripts and was an inveterate letter-writer.

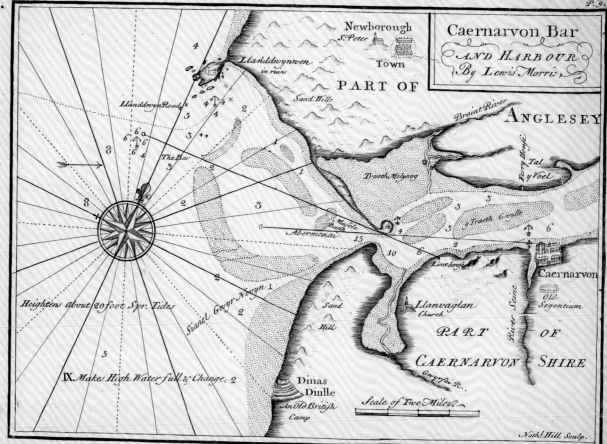

Caernarvon Bar
AND HARBOUR
By Lewis Morris,

Newborough
S.t Peter
Town

PART OF

ANGLESEY

Braint River

Ferry House
Tal
y Voel

Llanddwynwen
in ruins

Sand Hills

Traeth Melynog

Llanddwyn Road

y Traeth Gwillt

The Bar

Muscle
Bank

Abermenai

Lime house

Caernarvon

Old
Segontium

Llanvaglan
Church

Heightens about 20 foot Spr: Tides

Sianel Gwyr Newyn

Sand
Hills

PART OF

CAERNARVON SHIRE

Gwyrfai R.

IX Makes High Water full & Change 2

Dinas
Dinlle

An Old British
Camp

Scale of Two Miles.

Nath.l Hill Sculp.

Publish'd according to Act of Parliament Sep.t 29. 1748.

4·8 Japanned tray
c.1780

'Tom Allgood has found out a new way of Japanning, which I think is so beautiful that I will send you a few pieces of it.'

These words, written by Charles Hanbury Williams to his wife in 1734, mark the early beginnings of an industry based in Pontypool and later in Usk, whose products found their way across the world, from the court of Catherine the Great in Russia to revolutionary America. Japanning was the process of covering sheets of tinned iron with a resinous lacquer and painting the surface with ornamental designs.

The base of japanned ware was iron. The Torfaen valley was the site of some of the earliest iron-making in Wales. A bloomer furnace was producing iron for blacksmiths in the fifteenth century, heating local ironstone in a charcoal fire. Later, more powerful furnaces were using high-grade Osmond iron, and in 1576 Richard Hanbury, a London banker, founded a series of forges and furnaces in the valley. A descendant, John Hanbury, began using a rolling mill in Pontypool to produce thin iron sheets covered with tin. The scholar Edward Lhuyd reported in 1697: 'with these Plates he makes Furnaces, Pots, Kettles, Saucepans etc. These he can afford at a very cheap rate.'

By this time Thomas Allgood, a Quaker from Northamptonshire, had joined the Hanburys in Pontypool. His son Edward and grandson Thomas (Tom) perfected a method of coating tin sheets with a varnish that, on firing, produced a brilliant polish as the background for painted ornament. They kept the recipe of the coating process a well-guarded secret – visitors were forbidden from entering the workshop – and today it is hard to be certain exactly how the japanning effect was achieved. Probably the thin sheets were dipped in acid to clean them, before being cut into strips. The varnish was baked, and baked again after painting. The result was a rust-resistant object with a hard, brilliant surface.

The Allgoods began making japanned goods, including teapots and coffee pots, cheese and bread trays, bookends and snuff boxes, from a cottage in Trosnant. They had researched their market well. Art objects from China and Japan, especially varnished furniture, had appealed to European elites from the seventeenth century, and demand had spread. The business flourished, even after a rift in the Allwood family resulted in some members of the family leaving Pontypool to set up a rival factory in Usk. Japan ware was praised by Thomas Thomas in an ode he recited in a theatre in Pontypool:

They made the dross from scaly iron parts
The yielding sheets assume an endless form
And figures gay the polished black adorn.

This specially commissioned tray comes from the later period of the Pontypool workshop. Out of the intense black background bursts a brilliant array of flowers. The painting was designed and executed by one of a number of the plant's highly skilled limners, of whom Benjamin Barker was the best known.

Competition from factories in the English Midlands, able to turn out inferior but cheaper japanned ware, had a serious effect on the Welsh industry, and the use of electroplating from 1840 made traditional lacquering techniques obsolete. The Pontypool works closed in 1820, the Usk plant in 1860.

4.9 Parys Mountain tokens
1787-93

If a capitalist's ideal is to attack an existing monopoly, build a profitable business and defend it with a new monopoly, then Thomas Williams, the Copper King, was Wales's most successful early capitalist. According to the manufacturer Matthew Boulton, he was 'a perfect tyrant, [who] will screw damned hard when he has got anybody in his vice'.

Williams, born in Anglesey in 1737, trained as a lawyer. He helped a local landowner in a lawsuit about mining copper found in 1768 at Parys Mountain near Amlwch. In 1778 he was rewarded with a share of the lease of the mine. But he did more than exploit his lease. By setting up his own smelting and manufacturing plants at Holywell and Swansea he destroyed the cartel operating the Cornish copper mines. By 1787 he held a virtual monopoly of the British copper industry and controlled half of the world's copper trade. Though this power later waned, Williams kept his wealth and influence. At his death in 1802 his estate was worth half a million pounds.

Eventually most of Parys Mountain was mined, so that it was left a cratered and toxic landscape. Copper was extracted from the surface, from shallow shafts, by open-pit mining, and then by underground adits or shafts. The ore was broken into lumps to be transported, through the expanded port of Amlwch, to the smelter works. Artists like John Warwick Smith came from afar, anxious to record the sublime man-made pits, craters and chasms of the mountain.

A problem Thomas Williams faced was how to pay his workers, since the Royal Mint's coins at the time were too few and of poor quality. In 1787 he started minting his own, well-designed copper pennies (and later half-pennies). In all, over ten million tokens were minted, and had a wide circulation. On the penny's reverse was the monogram PMC (Parys Mining Company). The obverse showed the head of a hooded and bearded druid, surrounded by a wreath of oak leaves and acorns, a direct reference to the Anglesey druids recorded by Tacitus [5]. Druids were ubiquitous in eighteenth century Anglesey. Henry Rowlands gave them a leading role in the island's prehistory in his book *Mona antiqua restaurata* (1723), the Morris brothers [47] chose a druidic figure as a symbol of their new society, the Cymmrodorion [44], and the charitable Druidic Society of Anglesey was founded in 1772.

One of the main uses of Mynydd Parys copper was to sheathe the hulls of wooden ships, to prevent molluscs from boring into their timbers in tropical waters (hence the phrase 'copper-bottomed'). Many of these ships were implicated in the slave trade, and copper bangles, neptunes and kettles were shipped to Africa to exchange for slaves to be transported to the Caribbean. In July 1788 Thomas Williams petitioned Parliament to try to prevent the regulation of the slave trade. He claimed that government regulation would endanger his investment of £70,000 in factories producing goods that were 'entirely for the African market'.

Watercolour of Parys Mountain by John Warwick Smith (National Library of Wales)

50 Anti-slavery pamphlet
1792

By the end of the eighteenth century Carmarthen was the main centre for printing and publishing in Wales. Around 1792 John Daniel, the leading printer in the town, published a sixteen-page pamphlet, priced at one penny, written by an anonymous 'Welshman hostile to all oppression'. Its title, in translation, was *The sufferings of many thousands of black people, in wretched slavery in Jamaica and other places*, and its subtitle announced its aim: 'set out for the serious consideration of the amiable people of Wales, to try to persuade them to forsake sugar, treacle and rum'.

Boycotting Caribbean sugar was one of the main weapons of those determined to abolish the transatlantic slave trade. Britain had long been the world's biggest slave trading nation, and by the 1790s well over 200,000 slaves worked on Jamaica's sugar plantations. Welsh writers had already spoken out against the trade, notably the hymn-writer and Methodist leader William Williams Pantycelyn.

The pamphlet's author was Morgan John Rhys. Born near Llanbradach in 1760, he joined the Baptist denomination following his conversion and would become an itinerant minister. Nonconformists were often at the forefront of abolitionist campaigns, and like many of them Rhys combined missionary zeal with a burning sense of injustice. After the French Revolution broke out he crossed to France in August 1791. He rejoiced to see the Bastille in ruins, but his main activity was preaching the Protestant gospel, believing that Catholicism as well as tyranny could be defeated. Back in Wales in 1793, he set up the first political periodical in Welsh, *Y cylch-grawn Cynmraeg*, printed at the Methodists' press at Trefeca **[45]**. Its contents reflected

his radicalism and the breadth of his interests. Articles covered purifying religion, reforming the Welsh alphabet, science, the American revolution and the supposed Welsh Indians of North America.

In his pamphlet Rhys argues the need to explain the dire consequences of the sugar trade in the Welsh language, for those unable to read publications on the subject in English. The core of his argument is that slavery 'is unreasonable, unjust and wholly contrary to nature; something inconsistent with the obligations of the Christian religion and its instruction to love others as we love ourselves, and to do unto them as we would wish have them do unto us'. He goes on to describe the horrors of the slaves' transport to Jamaica and their treatment there.

The title page advertises a 'song' available from the same printer. This is a broadsheet in the form of twelve verses written as if by slaves, entitled, in translation, 'The complaints of black men in wretched slavery in the Sugar Islands'. This poem was probably also written by Rhys. Only one copy survives, in the personal papers of Iolo Morganwg **[18]**, who was also a fierce opponent of the slave trade.

In August 1794, as radical views met with government suppression, Rhys emigrated to the United States. He continued to attack slavery and defended the rights of native Americans. In 1795 he helped set up a black church in Savannah, Georgia, in the face of opposition by slave-owners. In 1796 he bought land in Pennsylvania, which he called Cambria. On it, in 1797, he founded a community called Beulah as a Welsh colony – one of many attempts, mostly unsuccessful, to transplant a part of Wales to the Americas **[64]**.

DIODDEFIADAU
MILOEDD LAWER
o
DDYNION DUON,

MEWN

Caethiwed Truenus yn JAMAICA a
Lleoedd eraill;

Yn cael eu gofod at YSTYRIAETH ddifrifol y
Cymry hawddgar, er mwyn ceifio eu hennill
i adael Suwgr, Triagl, a Rum.

Gan GYMRO, Gelynol i bob Gorthrech,

Yr hwn a ladrattao ddyn, ac a'i gwertho, neu os cair ef yn
ei law ef, rhoider ef i farwolaeth, Ecfod. xxi. 16.

En gwaedd hwynt a ddyrchafodd at Dduw, o blegid y
caethiwed, a Duw a glybu eu huchenaid hwynt, Ecfod.
ii. 23.

A ylaf fi waed y dynion hyn? 2 Cron. xi. 19.

CAERFYRDDIN,

ARGRAPHWYD AC AR WERTH YNO GAN IOAN DANIEL;
YN HEOL-Y-BRENIN;—MR. ROSS, YN HEOL-AWST;
MR. THO. MORGAN, WRTH Y FARCHNAD, YN ABER-
TAWE;—A MR. O. REES, YM MRISTO.—LLE GELLIR
CAEL AR WERTH CAN YN ERBYN ARFERYD SUWGR
PRIS DIMMEU.

(PRIS CEINIOG)

[1792]

51 Scold's bridle
1795

Poor people were a problem. From the sixteenth century governments tried to legislate to reduce their social cost. A common distinction, then as now, was between the 'impotent' poor (the unsupported old, disabled and children) who might deserve help, and others – able-bodied unemployed, vagrants and idlers – whose fate was control and punishment.

It was not until after 1750 that many parishes in Wales began to levy rates to provide for poor people, mainly through outdoor relief – grants of money, food or clothing. Workhouses, a more organised solution, were slow to develop. A parliamentary survey in 1777 found that there were 2,000 in England but only 19 in Wales – probably small, parish-based institutions. In 1795, following an Act of Parliament passed in 1792, the Montgomery and Pool Poor Law Union opened a workhouse in Forden. It was a large brick building, designed by Joseph Bromfield. It cost £12,000 and was intended to house up to 1,000 poor people from parishes in Montgomeryshire and Shropshire.

Forden's 'House of Industry' prevented its inmates from starving. It gave them some extremely basic education and medical care. But it was a place of harsh labour, poor sanitation and severe discipline, all designed to deter others from seeking its support. Infection and death were common. Men and women were segregated and set to hard physical work. Breaches of discipline brought stern punishment. On 20 May 1795 the official log records 'that Mary Hill be punished for her idleness (reprimanded); Grace Price for her disobedience (do.); Sarah Jones for her brutish behaviour (punished)'. 'Punishment' could involve public whippings, solitary confinement, being placed in stocks – and sometimes the scold's bridle. In May 1795 the directors resolved 'that a Bridle for Scolds and a Straight Waistcoat be procured for punishing Offending Poor in the House'.

First recorded as 'the branks' in sixteenth-century Scotland, the scold's bridle was already outdated by the end of the eighteenth century. It was an iron cage, fitted over the head, with a projecting plate that pressed down on the tongue to prevent speech. The bridle was thought to be a suitable penalty for disobedient or recalcitrant women. An entry from the official Forden record reads: 'Punishments - Ordered that Mary Davies wife of Robert Davies for riotous and other ill behaviour be confined with a Bridle for two hours'. On another occasion 'disorderly behaviour' condemned Anne Davies to the same penalty. The bridle was painful, but its real power lay in public humiliation. It was used only rarely on men. Its main intention was to reinforce male power by violently denying the right of women to express themselves.

Parliament passed a new law in 1834 which abolished 'out-relief' and made the workhouse even less attractive. Forden Workhouse, exempt from the new legislation, continued unreformed until 1870, 'a splendid receptacle of misery', to quote Rev. Emilius Nicholson, in his *Cambrian Traveller's Guide* (1840). The workhouse system was detested by residents, ratepayers, religious leaders and humanitarians. Hostility sometimes exploded. In Llanfair Caereinion in April 1837 an angry crowd attacked officials of the newly formed Llanfyllin Board of Guardians, including its chairman, Martin Williams. He was far from poor himself, as a local landowner and the beneficiary of a slave sugar plantation in Jamaica **[50]**.

52 Lord Penrhyn's slate quarry
1808

Richard Pennant, later 1st Baron Penrhyn, was a lucky man. In 1754 he inherited six Jamaican sugar plantations, first established by a Flintshire ancestor, Gifford Pennant of Holywell, and over 600 slaves. He kept an eye on his assets from afar. In a letter sent to Jamaica in 1783 he wrote: 'I am glad to hear the Negroes are well. The hearing a good account of them, and of the Cattle, always gives pleasure.' Pennant used his influence as an MP to wage a long campaign against abolition of the slave trade [50].

In 1765 he married, and through his wife gained part of the Penrhyn estate in Caernarfonshire. After acquiring the rest of the estate in the 1780s he used his sugar profits to transform the local slate industry. Small tenants, who paid a modest rent and royalties to mine their own slate, were bought out or driven away. Existing mines were gathered together to create a single quarry. Workers were directly employed, under the supervision of an agent.

Penrhyn dwarfed the earlier, small-scale mines scattered across the northern edge of Snowdonia. Pennant could see large profits in his slate as long as he could easily export it. He built a trackway from his quarry to the coast at the mouth of the river Cegin, later Port Penrhyn. In 1801 the track became one of the earliest narrow gauge railways in Britain. Slate was shipped to London, Bristol, Liverpool and Ireland, to help roof the houses of the rapidly growing towns and cities, and to make tombstones, paving stones and writing slates.

The quarry was excavated on a grand scale. By 1792, 500 men were producing 15,000 tons of slate a year. Slate seams appeared at the surface, and could be worked using broad open terraces or galleries as well as pits. Quarry work was strenuous and dangerous, while high levels of skill were needed to split and finish slates. In the classification invented by Pennant's father-in-law, slates were given female titles, like lady, duchess and empress, according to their size.

By the nineteenth century Penrhyn Quarry was such an awe-inspiring sight that tourists visited from afar. In 1807 the amateur topographical artist John Nixon arrived to record the great pits and cliffs of slate, with workers cutting slate and pushing trolleys on tracks. His illustration was reproduced as an etching in the *European magazine*. Other artists followed. Henry Hawkins painted a grandiose oil painting to commemorate a visit on 8 September 1832 by the 13-year-old Princess Victoria [58]. She wrote in her diary: 'It was very curious to see the men split the slate, & others cut it while others hung suspended by ropes and cut the slate; others again drove wedges into a piece of rock and in that manner would split off a block. We then got into our carriages and drove to Penrhyn castle, a most extraordinary building.' Penrhyn Castle, a neo-Norman mansion still unfinished in 1832, was built by the second Baron Penrhyn, George Hay Dawkins-Pennant, at a cost of around £150,000 (£50m in today's terms) to celebrate his power and success in extending his quarry.

Two years later Lord Penrhyn received a windfall. The Treasury paid him £14,682 as compensation for his loss of 764 slaves on four Jamaican sugar plantations, following the Slavery Abolition Act of 1833.

Drawn by J. Nixon Esq.

Engraved by S. Rawle.

LORD PENRYN'S SLATE QUARRY,

near Bangor, N. Wales.

53 Aberystwyth & Tregaron Bank notes
1810-14

Around 1810 John Evans, Joseph Jones and William Davies opened a bank in Aberystwyth. Starting a bank was not difficult, as long as sufficient capital was available. By 1797 230 banks had been set up outside London, in response to the growth and increasing complexity of local economies, and to the demand for a better flow of money and loans. The number had increased to 721 (about 40 in Wales) by 1810.

The men opened a Tregaron branch and their bank became known as the Aberystwyth & Tregaron Bank, or *Banc y Ddafad Ddu* after the black sheep that appeared on notes issued between 1810 and 1814. The £1 note showed a single sheep; two sheep appeared on the £2 note, and ten on the £10 note.

The choice of sheep was appropriate, since the bank reflected the main business of Cardiganshire, agriculture. Sheep and cattle were crucial to its economy. Some landowners were improvers, eager to increase the productivity of crops and stock – Thomas Johnes of Hafod was a constant experimenter – but most farms were traditional and small-scale. Good prices could be had for wool and meat while war with France continued, and Cardiganshire had an export economy.

Before the banks came, some of their functions were carried out by drovers. Drovers were critical to the cattle trade of mid Wales. They bought locally raised cattle at local fairs and walked them to the large markets in the English midlands and London. They used their own tracks to cross the inhospitable terrain of the Cambrian Mountains, including the route from Tregaron to Abergwesyn. Several Tregaron blacksmiths provided the cattle with shoes for the journey (400 might travel in the same drove). The drovers also took news, letters and printed material around the country, and carried money and bills to and fro across the English border. The sums they dealt in could be large, and their own earnings substantial.

In his book *Wild Wales* (1862) George Borrow recalled meeting an ex-drover near Tregaron and asking him whether he had long left the trade. 'Oh yes', came the answer, 'given him up a long time, ever since domm'd rail-road came into fashion'. In the 1880s the photographer John Thomas captured two of the last weather-beaten drovers of Montgomeryshire. Their names do not survive.

The end of the Aberystwyth and Tregaron Bank came much sooner. After warning about 'an attempt lately made to injure it by inveterate enemies', the undercapitalised bank went into liquidation in 1815. The end of the war with France that year brought an agricultural depression, made worse by a succession of poor harvests. Many banks failed, though *Banc yr Eidion Du* (the Black Ox Bank) in Llandovery survived until it was sold to Lloyds Bank in 1909. No valid Welsh banknotes have circulated since, despite an attempt by Richard Williams, suppressed by the government, to issue Welsh notes in 1968-69. Some of these bore the resonant words: 'The Black Sheep Company of Wales Limited'.

John Thomas, *Two drovers, Montgomery*
(National Library of Wales)

54. Potpourri vase
1815-1817

As copper-working developed along the banks of the river Tawe in Swansea in the eighteenth century, another, smaller industry grew up in its shadow. In 1764 William Coles, an ironmaster from Gloucester, founded a pottery, later called the Cambrian Pottery, on the west bank of the river. He produced coarse earthenware vessels for domestic use, using local clays. William's son John brought in a manager, George Haynes, who expanded and reorganised the pottery, engaging the services of specialists like the engraver Thomas Rothwell, the modeller George Bentley and the artist Thomas Pardoe.

In 1802 William Dillwyn, a Pennsylvania Quaker and well-known anti-slavery campaigner, bought the company for his son Lewis Weston Dillwyn. Lewis was a skilled botanist – in 1804 he was elected to the Royal Society for his published work on algae and shells. He became one of the founders in 1835 of the Swansea Philosophical and Literary Society (later the Royal Institution of South Wales), an important network of leading scientists and engineers based in the town. It was he who, in 1822, alerted William Buckland to the significance of the prehistoric finds in Paviland Cave [2].

In 1810 Lewis Weston Dillwyn, having learned pottery skills from Haynes, opened two new kilns and introduced new equipment. He imported clay and china stone from Cornwall, and, between 1814 and 1817, created translucent porcelain vessels of the finest quality. William Billingsley, a skilled artist who specialised in flower painting, came to Swansea from the porcelain factory at Nantgarw to help paint his wares.

The potpourri vase, intended to hold sweet-smelling herbs and flowers, is one of the most elaborate pieces to come from the Swansea China Works. It has two landscape scenes painted by Billingsley: Caerphilly Castle, and the bridge over the river Taff at Pontypridd built by William Edwards. The bridge was already recognised as one of the wonders of Wales. Edwards's first attempt, in 1746, was swept away by a flood. Finally, at the fourth attempt in 1756, Edwards succeeded. His bridge survives as a footbridge today.

William Edwards, born in Eglwysilan, taught himself masonry skills, in part by studying the stonework of Caerphilly Castle. Later he designed other bridges across south Wales, and three of his sons were also bridge builders. As a young man he came under the influence of Howell Harris [45]. In 1742, at the instigation of Harris and others, he built New House, the first purpose-built Methodist meeting house in Wales, at Waun Fach, Groes-wen, and was minister there for forty years.

When it was opened the new bridge at Pontypridd was thought to be the largest single span bridge in the world, with a graceful, steep curve to its crown and three circular voids on each side to reduce pressure on the centre. It was a magnet for visiting painters, including Richard Wilson, Julius Caesar Ibbetson and J.M.W. Turner. They showed it in a wholly rural setting. The author Benjamin Heath Malkin visited in 1803 and wrote of the 'stupendous bridge', the 'luxuriance of the hanging woods' and the 'hills which close in upon the river'. Pontypridd, still called Newbridge, did not begin to develop as a town until the Brown Lenox chainworks was set up in 1816. Its population remained modest until the 1880s, when it became the front door to the booming coalmining industry in the Rhondda and Taff valleys.

55 Riots in Merthyr
1816

According to the economist Walter Davies, Merthyr Tydfil in 1750 'exhibited no symptoms of its subsequent wealth and population, more than other mountainous villages in the Glamorgan coal tract'. Suddenly, thanks to iron, it found itself at the heart of the industrial revolution. By 1811 over 11,000 people lived there, making it the most populous parish in Wales. Merthyr had seventeen iron furnaces, producing 30,000 tons of pig iron. Iron ore, limestone and coal were abundant, and the industry was stimulated by the invention in the 1780s of the Welsh method of puddling to make malleable iron.

People flooded to the ironworks of Merthyr from Wales and beyond. There was ample work for skilled puddlers, rollers and furnacemen as well as labourers. Demand for iron from industry and the armed forces increased, until the end of the Napoleonic wars brought economic depression. Employers threatened to cut wages, and in summer 1816 the price of corn rose sharply on the prospect of a poor harvest.

Discontent increased in Merthyr and turned to desperation. Trade unions did not yet exist: action took the form of strikes, threats, riots and violence against the employers' agents and property. In October 1816 a crowd of workers moved from works to works, putting the blast furnaces out of action. In Merthyr they chased away the police and threatened the employers and their managers. Soldiers arrived, but the crowd had already left to incite strikes in other towns. The rioters returned to the town to find men of the 55th Regiment and the Swansea Cavalry. After a cavalry charge peace was restored without bloodshed, and several men were tried and imprisoned.

Penry Williams's painting shows the arrival of the 55th Regiment and the Swansea Cavalry near the Castle Inn. Redcoats hold their bayonets and pikes aloft; people flee at the approach of other troops; cavalry gallop behind. Williams was fourteen years old when he painted the scene. His talent was recognised by the main ironworks owner in Merthyr, William Crawshay, who may have helped arrange his art training in London.

Williams made several paintings of Crawshay's properties, including his home, Cyfarthfa Castle, and the Cyfarthfa ironworks, reputed to be the largest ironworks in the world. Williams's 1825 scene of the ironworks at night shows workers transporting and working the metal. Through the open side of the building can be seen Cyfarthfa Castle, newly completed at a cost of £30,000. According to its architect, Robert Lugar, the works 'at night offer a truly magnificent scene, resembling the fabled Pandemonium'.

Workers' resistance to their conditions and to their treatment at the hands of their employers continued. Merthyr's radical culture was strengthened towards the end of the 1820s by increasing demands for political reform. In 1831 disaffection, sparked in part by a reduction on wages imposed by Crawshay, exploded in a serious and bloody revolt, the Merthyr Rising, which saw the first use of the red flag as a symbol of rebellion and Wales's first working class martyr, Richard Lewis, or Dic Penderyn.

Penry Williams, Cyfarthfa ironworks
(Cyfarthfa Castle Museum and Art Gallery)

56 The Nannau ox
1824

On 25 June 1824 the heir of the 12,000-acre Nannau estate in Merioneth, Robert Williames Vaughan, was twenty-one years old. To mark his coming of age, his father, also called Robert Williames Vaughan, ordered public celebrations.

A newspaper reported the preparations:

'At day break in the morning 21 rounds of guns were fired off from Cader Idris, which were returned from guns placed on eminences near Nannau. At the same early hour, the bells of Dolgelly steeple commenced ringing an harmonious peal, and continued during the whole of the day. The bugles and trumpets of the Merionethshire militia struck up the revalley, and continued playing martial and other airs; flags were displayed on the towers of the church, and in different parts of the town.

'At one o'clock a grand procession was formed, which proceeded from Dolgelley to Nannau, consisting of a great number of respectable gentlemen on horseback, followed by an innumerable multitude on foot; next followed an elegant mail coach drawn by four beautiful brown horses, richly decorated with laurel and ribbons.'

They were welcomed at Nannau, where a special tent had been erected to accommodate 200 diners (a new kitchen wing had been added to the house earlier). Three hundred others sat to dinner elsewhere. After the fish course they enjoyed slices from a valuable white oxen weighing 165 pounds, presented by the estate's cowman, Sion Dafydd. Wine and beer flowed freely.

To commemorate the event a painting of the ox with Sion Dafydd was commissioned from the artist Daniel Clowes of Chester. The ox's horns and hooves were later incorporated into an elaborate candelabrum. Six special toasting cups were also ordered, made from the wood of *Derwen Ceubren yr Ellyll*, The Hollow Oak of the Demon, an ancient tree at Nannau in which, according to popular tradition, Owain Glyndŵr [25] had his treacherous cousin Hywel Sele incarcerated. The Welsh inscription around the silver rim of one of them reads, in translation: 'While the sun shines on Cadair Idris may there be a welcome in Nannau, and Robert Fychan to arrange it'.

'Gentlemen' were not the only beneficiaries of Sir Robert Vaughan's generosity. Other oxen were roasted at Corwen, Barmouth and Bala, and the poor of the area invited to taste the beef, washed down with ale. Fireworks were let off, and at Dolgellau a hot air balloon made an ascent.

Vaughan was one of the last of the great landowners who, despite his social and political conservatism, felt responsibility for his tenants and shared in their culture. All his instincts were reactionary. He was against Catholics, parliamentary reform and the abolition of slavery. But he was a half-hearted politician: in his 44 years as MP for Merioneth he made only one speech in the House of Commons. He was much more comfortable at home in Wales. His house at Nannau was open to all, and he patronised Welsh poets, one of whom, Meurig Idris, wrote a long eulogy to him when he died in 1843.

Robert Williames Vaughan the son lacked the qualities of his father. He also lacked an heir, and when he died in 1859 the estate was broken up. The old tradition of deference and patronage was at an end. Political reform was under way, and economic change meant that money counted for more than family history and land inheritance.

57 Neath Abbey beam engine
1824

Cornwall was the original home of several of south Wales's industrial pioneers. Around 1800 John Vivian moved from Truro to manage copper works at Penclawdd and Loughor. Richard Trevithick, from a village near Camborne, was responsible for the world's first steam-driven locomotive journey, from Penydarren to Abercynon, in 1804.

Earlier, in 1792, a group of Quakers from Falmouth had founded the Neath Abbey Iron Company. Their initial aim was to make iron components for pumping engines in Cornish tin mines. A visitor in 1798 saw 'two immense blast furnaces .... constantly at work, each of them producing upwards of thirty tons of pig iron every week'. The company became known for the high quality and extreme precision of its work. It expanded its product range, as the demands of industry grew, to include steam locomotives and machines for water and gas works, as well as pumping and winding engines used in mines.

One of Neath Abbey's specialities was ship engines. In June 1824 'a numerous and very respectable company of gentlemen and ladies' made an excursion on the new paddlewheel steamship *Lord Beresford* in Swansea Bay. 'The vessel', the *Cambrian* newspaper reported, 'is extremely elegant in appearance, and has very superior and spacious accommodations. She has two excellent engines, of above 60 horse power each, manufactured by the *Neath Abbey Company*, under the superintendence of H. Price, Esq., which propel her along at the rate of 10 or 11 miles an hour, without producing any unpleasant sensation.'

By now Henry Habberley Price owned the Neath Abbey company, with his brother Joseph Tregelles Price.

A satirical poem by Edward Pease gives a flavour of Joseph's dedication and professionalism:

> Joseph Price, Joseph Price,
> Thou art mighty precise,
> Methought t'other night in a dream
>
> That thou really walked
> Slept, ate, drank, and talked,
> And prayed every Sunday by steam.

The company's reputation earned it contracts overseas. In February 1824 the *Cambrian* reported that 'considerable contracts have been entered into within the last fortnight for steam engines and other machinery by the Anglo-Mexican Mining Association. The Neath Abbey Company, Messrs Walker and Co. of Staffordshire and Mr. George Stephenson, of Newcastle, we understand, are the contractors'. The detailed plan and elevation of a 53-inch single beam engine designed at Neath Abbey under this contract is preserved in a rare collection of early engineering drawings.

On 4 March 1825 the *Rosalind* sailed from Swansea bound for Mexico, laden with the finished machinery and forty mechanics and miners. A newspaper reported: 'The sympathetic feeling shewn by the assembled multitude on the pier for their success and happiness must have been highly gratifying to these brave adventurers'. One of those on board was David Williams, the Anglo-Mexican Mining Association's agent. His letters to Swansea give a vivid picture of the long journey, the silver mines at Guanajuato and life in Mexico: he regretted there were neither 'pretty girls to dress our food, nor one drop of good ale such as you have at Landore'.

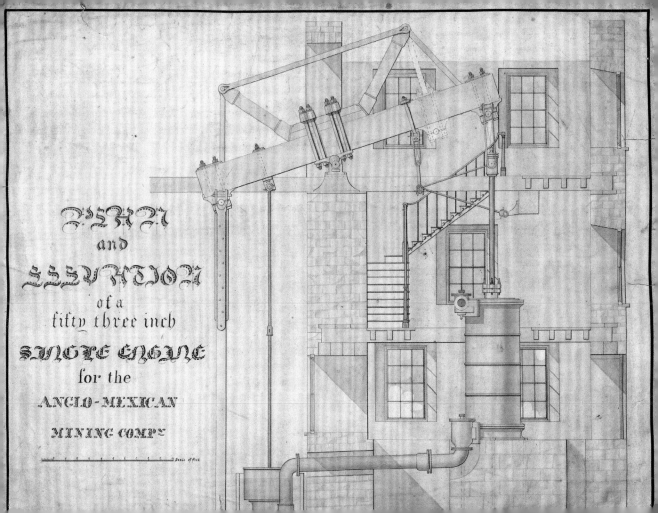

PLAN
and
ELEVATION
of a
fifty three inch
SINGLE ENGINE
for the
ANGLO-MEXICAN
MINING COMPY

Scale of Feet

58 Welsh hat
c.1830

An enduring symbol of Welsh women and girls in popular representation is the Welsh hat. Around 180 original examples survive in museums. Little, though, can be said with certainty about the hat's history and uses.

There are two versions, both with tall crowns and stiff, flat brims. One has a tapering crown; the other type, used in north-west Wales, is shorter and more cylindrical. The earliest ones were made of felt, but most surviving examples were made of silk plush, known as 'beaver', on a stiff buckram base. Most of these were made by two English companies, Christys and Carver and Co., specifically for the Welsh market. They were expensive and were probably worn by better-off rural women, on special occasions.

The origin of the hat is unknown. Tall felt hats were worn by seventeenth century Puritans, but they fell into disuse. Early travellers in Wales noted that women often wore men's hats. The Welsh hat emerged in the early 1830s. Princess Victoria, passing through Bangor in August 1832 [52], 'appeared, in compliment to the fair maids of Cambria, in the head-dress of the country, the Welsh hat'. It is possible that her example was influential. The American writer Nathaniel Hawthorne wrote after visiting north Wales in 1854, 'many of the Welsh women, particularly the older ones, wear black beaver hats, high crowned and almost precisely like men's. It makes them look ugly and witch-like.'

In 1834 Augusta Hall, Lady Llanover [59], won first prize in a Cardiff eisteddfod for an essay urging the preservation of the Welsh language and the 'national costume of Wales', which included the 'neat and serviceable beaver hat'. A set of drawings of Welsh women wearing different regional costumes was published at the same time, showing the *betgwn* or gown, but none wears the Welsh hat. She was not responsible for inventing the Welsh hat, but Lady Llanover anticipated its transition from icon of tradition to symbol of national identity. By the 1860s the hats had ceased to be worn unselfconsciously. Women wearing them were photographed in studio or staged settings.

Arguably it was the English, not the Welsh, who elevated the hat-and-shawl into a national symbol. In 1909 the Port Sunlight soap magnate Lord Leverhulme bought a watercolour, *Salem*, by an English painter, Sydney Curnow Vosper, and gave away prints of it in exchange for tokens from bars of Sunlight soap. This popular picture, set in the Baptist chapel at Pentre Gwynfryn, Ardudwy, established a powerful but outdated image of traditional Wales, with its rural setting, Nonconformist chapel, deep piety and, most striking, its Welsh hat and shawl. Siân Owen, the central figure, conformed to a commonplace Welsh image, the strong, stern matriarch. In popular imagery, as in the newspaper cartoons of J.M. Staniforth, this stereotype had already begun to appear as the symbol of the nation, Dame Wales, accompanied by tall hat and shawl. She often represented traditional Welsh moral authority. In an 1889 cartoon she chides the town of Cardiff, 'Shame on you – running your 'buses on Sunday!' She could also voice more a nationalistic opinion. In 1895, when Birmingham Corporation was building the Elan reservoirs, she confronts a spade-carrying Englishman, 'Coming to carry away the water from my mountains, ar' you! Very kind indeet, look you. But please to remember, sar, that I shall have a voice in that matter.'

59 Abergavenny Eisteddfod medal
1834

In 1823 Augusta Waddington, English heiress of the Llanover estate near Abergavenny, married Benjamin Hall of Abercarn (Big Ben is supposedly named after him, from his period as commissioner of works during the building of the Houses of Parliament). Fifteen years later, when her husband was made a baronet, she became known as Lady Llanover. She hardly conformed to the model of the dutiful, aristocratic matron. Rather, she was a 'violent Welshwoman', to quote one of her admirers – determined to promote, with energy and determination, all things Welsh, especially the Welsh language and traditional culture.

Augusta was close to a friend of her mother, Lady Elisabeth Coffin Greenly, a fluent Welsh-speaker, musician and patron of Iolo Morganwg [18]. In 1826 Augusta met Thomas Price, known as Carnhuanawc, historian, orator and cultural entrepreneur, and one of a group of Anglican clergy devoted to Welsh-language culture. Under their influence she learnt Welsh and flung herself into many activities. She employed Welsh speakers at Llanover Court, supported the first Welsh-language periodical for women, *Y Gymraes*, and funded two Welsh-medium schools in Llanover and the Welsh Collegiate Institute in Llandovery. She played the harp, advocated the use of the Welsh triple harp, and promoted traditional Welsh music. She urged the preservation of Welsh women's dress [58] and set up a woollen mill on her estate.

In 1834 Lady Llanover joined the Abergavenny Cymreigyddion Society, formed the year before by Thomas Price and others with the intention of arranging eisteddfodau. The eisteddfod, with poets and musicians competing for prizes, already had a long but discontinuous history. Gruffudd ap Nicolas held an eisteddfod at Carmarthen in around 1450, and others followed at Caerwys in 1523 and 1567. More informal (and beery) gatherings in the eighteenth century were followed by an eisteddfod in Llangollen in 1789, and between 1809 and 1834 provincial eisteddfodau were held around Wales by four Cambrian societies. The Cymreigyddion held their first, modest eisteddfod in 1834, the first of ten held up to 1853. Prizes were awarded for poetry and literature. The prize for an essay on 'The History of Gwent Before the Romans' was awarded to Eiddil Ifor, the pen-name of Thomas Evan Watkins. His medal shows a prehistoric warrior, lightly clad but heavily armed. Standing in front of a landscape with cromlech, he holds a spear, sword, bow and arrows, and a small round shield reminiscent of a medieval buckler [29].

In time the Abergavenny eisteddfodau grew in size. By the fourth, in 1837, Lady Llanover had attracted a large number of the aristocracy and gentry, some of whom sponsored the 34 competitions. Prize money totalled 150 guineas. Lady Greenly offered a prize for the best collection of unpublished Welsh music. The winner was Maria Jane Williams, and her work, the first published collection of Welsh folk songs, appeared in 1844, with help from Lady Llanover and others, as *Ancient National Airs of Gwent and Morganwg*.

In the 1848 eisteddfod the Prince of Wales prize was won by a chemist from Merthyr Tydfil, Thomas Stephens, for the first scholarly dissertation on medieval Welsh literature, later published as *The Literature of the Kymry*. Stephens was in touch with academics from France and Germany, many of whom were invited to Llanover Court. A Breton delegation attended the 1838 eisteddfod – a foretaste of the later pan-Celtic movement.

60 Portraits of industrial workers
c.1835

'Poor creatures broiling all in sweat and dirt, amid their furnaces, pits and rolling mills ... 50,000 grimy mortals, black and clammy ... screwing out a living for themselves'. Thomas Carlyle, who visited Merthyr in 1850, saw the industrial workers of the town as an undifferentiated mass of suffering humanity. But an unusual series of sixteen small portraits shows some of them as real people, with individual features and distinctive attributes.

The pictures, probably painted by itinerant artist William Jones Chapman, were commissioned in about 1835 by the ironmaster Francis Crawshay. Francis was the son of William Crawshay II, who built Cyfarthfa Castle [55]. William seems to have regarded him as less reliable than his other son, Robert Thompson, and entrusted him with the control of two of his lesser enterprises, the iron works at Hirwaun in the Cynon Valley and a new tinplate works at Treforest. According to tradition, Francis was an unusual employer. He refused to live in the owner's house at Hirwaun, preferring to occupy a small house near the works. He took an interest in his workers, teaching himself Welsh so that he could talk to them easily. They in turn called him 'Mr Frank'.

The portraits are all of named men employed either at Hirwaun or at Treforest. (There are no women, who would certainly have been employed too.) They include supervisory as well as skilled and unskilled manual workers. Among the occupations listed are quarryman, finery worker, mechanic, carpenter, storekeeper, lodge keeper, tin mills manager and mine agent. Their faces are those of recognisable individuals, their clothes reflect their occupation, and they sometimes carry the tools of

their trade. All of them are painted with dignity and respect. David Davies, in his waistcoat and jacket and broad-brimmed hat, is a cinder-filler at the Hirwaun ironworks. He carries a long shovel, and smoke rises behind him from the hot coals. William James, dressed in cap and kerchief, is described as a 'roller' at the Treforest works. He carries a pair of large grippers to hold the tinplate sheets, and wears a thick apron to protect himself from the hot and pliant metal.

In 1836 Francis Crawshay moved to a new home, Forest House, in Treforest, to be close to the growing tinplate works. But his dedication to running the business was half-hearted, and he preferred other interests. These included traditional upper-class pursuits like hunting, but also more eccentric ones. About 1848 he built a circular stone tower above Hirwaun, sometimes called a 'folly', though he may have planned it as a refuge in case of a repetition of the riots of 1831 [55] and the Chartist uprising of 1839 [61]. In Treforest he befriended the eccentric Dr William Price of Llantrisant, who acted as a medical adviser to the Crawshay family. Price was a highly unVictorian figure, a Chartist who opposed marriage, Christianity, meat-eating and tobacco smoking. In 1884 he caused a sensation by cremating the body of his son, Iesu Grist (Jesus Christ). He aimed to revive the religion of the Druids [49], inventing traditions and regalia to support his case. Francis Crawshay set up his own druidic circle near Forest House; in his will he forbade one of his sons from demolishing it, on pain of losing his share of the inheritance.

61 John Frost's pistols
1839

On the night of Sunday 3 November 1839 about 3,000 Chartist workers, armed with guns, pikes, knives and cudgels, streamed down the Sirhowy and Ebbw valleys in three columns to converge on Newport. One group, led by innkeeper Zephaniah Williams, started in Nant-y-glo, John Frost's group came from Blackwood, and William Jones, a watch-maker, led a third from Pontypool.

This was the beginning of the Newport Rising, the most acute confrontation between workers and state in nineteenth century Britain. The marchers were already suffering from the effects of economic depression, exploitation by their employers and the oppression of the poor law [51]. They were further inflamed by the government's opposition to the demands of Chartist leaders for radical political reform, such as voting rights for all men, a secret ballot and annual parliaments. In Wales Chartism found fertile ground. In Carmarthen the lawyer Hugh Williams founded the Working Men's Association in 1837. Morgan Williams was active in Merthyr and Dr William Price in Pontypridd [60]. Led by Thomas Powell, Chartists forcibly occupied Llanidloes for five days in April 1839. The main figure in south-east Wales was John Frost, a draper and former mayor of Newport, well known in radical circles in London.

The Newport marchers aimed to frighten the authorities into releasing Henry Vincent, the Chartist leader, and Newport Chartists who had been detained in the Westgate Hotel. More radical leaders, like Zephaniah Williams, wanted to capture and occupy Newport and the coalfield towns and hold them against the government. The approach to Newport on the morning of 4 November was poorly co-ordinated and the campaign in the town chaotic. When the crowd formed in front of the Westgate Hotel soldiers opened fire. At least twenty Chartists were killed. Their leaders were captured and tried for high treason. When Frost was arrested, a newspaper reported, 'he handed from his pockets three new pistols, about fifty bullets, and a flask of powder'. At a special session in Monmouth in December 1839 eight of the defendants were found guilty and condemned to death. After loud protests the government agreed to commute the sentences. Five were imprisoned and Williams, Jones and Frost were transported to Van Diemen's Land (Tasmania). In 1856 Frost was allowed to return to Britain. Still a radical, he spoke in Merthyr in 1857 about the evils of transportation.

The defeat of the Newport insurrection and an economic upturn in the 1840s did not signal the end of Chartism in Wales. In Merthyr, Morgan Williams continued to campaign. The town took part in a general strike in 1842, and even in the 1850s meetings were held and petitions signed. In April 1870 William Gould, a veteran Merthyr Chartist, unveiled his newly invented mechanical vote-counting box, an attempt to mechanise one of the Chartists' central demands, a secret ballot. 'It is certainly a very ingenious piece of mechanism', said the *Merthyr Telegraph*; 'Mr Simons, however, found a flaw in the operation of the system'. Gould's machine was never adopted.

William Gould's ballot box
(Cyfarthfa Castle Museum and Art Gallery)

62 'Baptism at Llanbadarn'
c.1840

The first Baptist congregation in Wales was set up by John Miles in the village of Ilston, Gower in 1649. Once the Commonwealth came to an end, Baptists, like other nonconformists, were persecuted for their beliefs. Many emigrated to North America. Miles sailed to New England and founded the town of Swansea, Massachussetts **[63]**. Other Baptists remained. By 1800 there were 60 chapels; by 1851, 533.

For Baptists personal commitment to Christ was symbolised by their characteristic ritual of adult baptism through total immersion. Each congregation appointed its own ministers and officers, without oversight by external clergy. This democratic spirit could lead members to take radical positions, like that of Morgan John Rhys on slavery and revolution **[50]**. Towards the end of the eighteenth century, under the influence of the growing Methodist movement, Baptists adopted a passionate evangelical style, and provided many of the celebrity preachers who drew large crowds across Wales.

The acknowledged star among these was Christmas Evans. Evans, born near Llandysul in 1776, began as an illiterate farm servant, and lost his left eye in a brawl. He was converted in 1783, joined the Baptists and became a minister in Llŷn and Anglesey. His preaching style was dramatic and imaginative. Large numbers came to hear him. His remaining eye, according to one biographer, 'could light an army through a wilderness on a dark night'. His manner could be fierce. According to another biographer, 'a shallow atheist was ridiculing the idea of a God, because, as he alleged, he had no sensible evidence of his being. Mr. Evans answered, "My friend, the mole in the meadow has never seen a king; shall he therefore say there is no king? O thou atheistic mole!"' Evans died in 1838, but his name was still celebrated decades later, when Staffordshire figurines of him sat in the houses of the pious.

'Baptism at Llanbadarn' was painted in about 1840. It shows an adult baptism in the river Rheidol near Llanbadarn Fawr near Aberystwyth. The figures are dressed in their finery; most of the women wear Welsh hats **[58]** and one carries a parasol. One woman stands mid-stream, waiting to be immersed, probably by the minister of Moriah Baptist chapel, about a mile distant.

The anonymous painter was responsible for fifty-eight other paintings of equal interest. He or she was a non-professional artist, but a remarkably sensitive colourist with a sure grasp of composition and attention to detail. Other scenes include rivers, harbours, bridges, castles, churches and mills, often in and around Aberystwyth, and feature fishermen, farmers and women workers.

In 1996 Gwyneth Lewis published 'Bedydd yn Llanbadarn', a poem inspired by the painting. Her 'Margaret Ann' stands in the river:

> As the river closed
> above her head,
> Margaret Ann heard the roar
> of salmon breathing
> and the water's weight,
> its turbulent history,
> a bond between her
> and the minister.

**Figurine of Christmas Evans
(Amgueddfa Cymru - National Museum Wales)**

63 Figurehead from the *Governor Fenner*
1841

On 24 February 1841 the sailing ship *Governor Fenner* set out from Liverpool for New York. On board were 18 crew and 107 passengers, mainly emigrants from Ireland. At 2.20am, fifteen miles off Holyhead, it struck a paddle-steamer, the *SS Nottingham*, broke in two and almost immediately sank. Only the captain and the first mate survived. The next day a steamer came across the bow section of the wreck floating off the Skerries islands, and retrieved parts of it, including the ship's figurehead. Captain Andrews of the *Governor Fenner* was later censured because his ship was showing no lights at the time of the collision. The ship was described as 'rotten as a pear' and 'old and crazy and unsound'.

The *Governor Fenner* had been built in Swansea, Massachussetts **[62]** in 1827. It was owned at one time by the DeWolfs of Rhode Island, who had gained their wealth from the slave trade, and was also used for whaling before becoming an emigrant ship.

The ship's figurehead was not carved from a single block of wood, as was usual in Britain, but formed from nine vertical planks of wood, glued and bolted together. American figureheads often featured images of prominent political figures, in this case James Fenner, a Governor of Rhode Island. In 2014 conservators restored the figurehead and repainted it in accordance with the style of surviving examples.

Welsh coast shipping routes became busier in the nineteenth century, with increases in trade and emigration, especially to America. Despite better maps and navigation aids **[47]** the coast remained a highly dangerous place. In stormy or foggy weather ships could hit rocks and reefs, like the Skerries off Anglesey, or become stranded on sand bars and beaches, like Cefn Sidan in Carmarthenshire. During the nineteenth century 100 shipwrecks occurred on average each year, with an average of 78 sailors killed. This was despite the growth of lighthouses. The Skerries lighthouse, one of the earliest lighthouses in Wales, was built by William Trench in 1717. Trench's plan was to extract payments from ships due to pass his lighthouse, but he found it impossible to collect them and died in debt. Trinity House finally gained control of the light in 1841. By the 1860s it had organised lighthouses to guard all of the critical points of the Welsh coast.

Shipping provided Welsh coastal communities with abundant employment – as captains and ships' crew, shipbuilders and, later, dockworkers. A glance at monuments outside churches in Aberdaron in Llŷn or Llansanffraid in Ceredigion shows that almost every family in some villages depended on the sea for a living, with mariners travelling to South America and other distant destinations. In Llansanffraid over 50 wooden vessels were built between 1786 and 1864 (some of the larger ships were towed to Aberystwyth to be rigged there); about half were later wrecked. The river Mawddach, today totally rural, was a major centre of shipbuilding: between 1750 and 1865, 318 vessels were constructed at yards in Penmaenpool and sailed downriver to be finished and registered at Barmouth.

The growth of the coal exporting ports of Cardiff and Barry from the 1880s created thousands of new maritime jobs, and attracted seamen from around the world. Many of them settled, and Butetown in Cardiff became one of the first substantial multi-ethnic communities in Britain **[83]**.

64. The good brig Credo
1848

What were you to do if you were a small tenant farmer in Cardiganshire in the mid-nineteenth century, without the means to make ends meet? There were two obvious choices. One was to migrate to an industrial area elsewhere in Wales or in England, where jobs were available and earnings higher. The other was to emigrate to America and to farm there – a solution advocated by Samuel Roberts, the radical writer and scourge of oppressive Welsh landlords, who himself tried to found a Welsh settlement in east Tennessee in 1857.

The 'good brig' *Credo*, owned by the Jones family of Aberystwyth, offered to take emigrants from that town to Quebec for £3 5s for each adult and £1 12s 6d for each child. The ship, which could carry 200 passengers, made the same journey regularly starting in 1836, returning to Aberystwyth from North America with cargoes of timber. It is unlikely that many of the emigrants on board in April 1848 intended to make Canada their home. It was simply that the passage to British North America was cheaper than sailing to New York: most emigrants made the overland journey south to where their compatriots had already settled in the United States.

The burden of transporting a family was high, once maintenance costs were added ('passengers to find their own provisions, etc.') and money set aside for settling in America. The voyage was long (perhaps seven weeks), cramped and uncomfortable, with few medical facilities on board. In newspapers the *Credo*'s captain, John Humphreys, recommended 'Humphreys' Tonic Aperient Pills, a most esteemed remedy for bilious and liver complaints, and other disorders of the stomach and bowels'. This medicine, he claimed, had restored the ship's carpenter to full health when all other remedies had failed.

The pressures to leave were strong. Agriculture was the main occupation of most Cardiganshire people. But even when supplemented with other work, like mining lead or knitting stockings, farming seldom yielded more than a small surplus, even in favourable economic times. When prices were low and harvests failed, many families, especially in upland areas like Mynydd Bach in central Cardiganshire, felt they had no choice but to migrate. Emigration from the county to America reached its height between the 1830s and 1850s.

Cardiganshire settlers tended to cluster in particular locations in the United States, like Waukesha County in Wisconsin and Jackson and Gallia counties in Ohio, which for a time was known as 'Little Cardiganshire'. In part they were guided by those who had gone before. In Aberystwyth in 1837 Rev. Edward Jones of Cincinnati published his pamphlet *Y Teithiwr Americanaidd* (The American Traveller), a practical guide for prospective emigrants to the US, 'those whom the wheel of providence, in its wisdom, has turned against'.

Emigration to America, though, was on a relatively small scale, and although many more workers left the county's farms to make a living in the south Wales coalfield in the later part of the century, Cardiganshire's overall population increased gradually between 1840 and 1880, before declining in subsequent decades. Only since the 1980s has its population increased substantially.

Memory of the *Credo* is still alive. In 2002 Mari Rhian Owen published her play written for the theatre company Arad Goch, *The Good Brig Credo*. She was inspired by the poster to imagine the feelings of the emigrants on board the ship.

TO
PARTIES DESIROUS OF EMIGRATING
To AMERICA.

18  48.

THE GOOD

BRIG CREDO,

Of Aberystwyth, John Humphreys, Master,

WILL SAIL FROM THAT PORT (WEATHER PERMITTING)

FOR QUEBEC DIRECT,

On the 4th of April next,

And will take PASSENGERS upon the following terms and conditions :—

	£	s.	d.		s.	d.	
Adults, 14 years of age and upwards -	3	0	0	with 5	0	head money	
Children, 1 year and under 14 of age -	1	10	0	„ 2	6	„	„
Infants, under 12 months - - - - -	Free.						

Passengers to find their own Provisions, &c., and the Ship will find Water, Fuel, and Bed Places.

As a limited number only will be engaged, the Passage should be secured by the 13th of March at the latest, at which time a deposit of £2 for each Adult, and £1 each Child must be made, which will be forfeited in the event of the Passenger declining the Voyage. The Passengers to be on board not later than Monday, the 3rd of April, when they will be required to pay the remainder of the Passage Money, and the Head Money.

Any further information that may be required, can be obtained on application to Mr Thomas Jones, at the Ropewalk, or to the Master on board.

J. COX, PRINTER AND STATIONER, PIER STREET, ABERYSTWYTH

65 Dame Venedotia sousing the spies
1848

In 1847 the government published a report, of 1,252 closely printed pages, entitled *Reports of the Commissioners of Inquiry into the state of education in Wales*. In Wales it provoked an outburst of indignation. Among the responses was a satirical play by R. J. Derfel, *Brad y Llyfrau Gleision*, and the 'treachery of the Blue Books' is the phrase attached to the report ever since.

It was a Welshman from Carmarthenshire, William Williams, MP for Coventry, who persuaded the British government to inquire into education in Wales, 'especially the means afforded to the labouring classes of acquiring a knowledge of the English language'. Three Commissioners were sent from London. They were thorough in gathering statistics and evidence, but they were young and inexperienced; they knew little about teaching or Wales, and nothing of the Welsh language.

Their report exposed in great detail the inadequacies of elementary education throughout the country. There were too few schools, in general teachers provided a poor quality of education, and illiteracy was common. But it was what the commissioners said about Wales and the Welsh in general that angered so many. Their writing shifted easily from analysis into moral condemnation. Poverty they regarded as a symptom of moral degeneracy. They complained of a long list of sins: 'petty thefts, lying, cozening, every species of chicanery, drunkenness and idleness, and want of chastity in the women', supporting their allegations with quotations by numerous ministers of religion (hence the 'treachery' of R.J. Derfel). They associated immorality with social resistance and political rebelliousness: 'The morals of the population congregated at and near Brynmawr and Beaufort are deplorably low. Drunkenness, blasphemy,

indecency, sexual vices and lawlessness, widely prevail there. This district was one of the chief sources of Chartism [61].' As for the people's language, 'the Welsh language is a vast drawback to Wales, and a manifold barrier to the moral progress and commercial prosperity of the people. It is not easy to over-estimate its evil effects … It dissevers the people from intercourse which would greatly advance their civilisation, and bars the access of improving knowledge to their minds. As a proof of this, there is no Welsh literature worthy of the name.'

The reaction in Wales was furious. Nonconformists used the many critical quotations from Anglican clergy in the report to paint themselves as the only true defenders of the nation. But many of them also used its damning conclusions as evidence that moral, religious and linguistic reform was urgent. Temperance became a priority, and the English language a road to social acceptance.

One of the nonconformists who responded most viscerally to the report was an artist from Llandudno, Hugh Hughes. He was an accomplished landscapist, but specialised in portraits of ministers and members of the expanding nonconformist middle class. In 1823 he illustrated the first Welsh magazine for children, *Yr Addysgydd*. A political radical and a maverick, he contributed a series of ten biting cartoons, 'Pictures for the million of Wales', to *The Principality*, published in 1848 by his friend Evan Jones (Ieuan Gwynedd), a leading Blue Books critic. One of them shows Wales as a woman, with a Welsh hat [58] and costume, dropping the three commissioners or 'spies' into the Irish Sea. The cartoons proved powerful, and Dame Venedotia (Mrs Gwynedd), an ancestor of Wales as a mother figure, was often reprinted and adapted.

66 John Roberts's triple harp

c.1850

The triple harp was an Italian classical concert instrument. From the seventeenth century it was taken up enthusiastically by Welsh harpists working in a more domestic tradition. It was this triple harp or *telyn deires*, and not the older, simpler harp played since medieval times, that became known as the Welsh harp. It continued to be played, mainly in north Wales, long after it fell out of fashion elsewhere. Instead of having a single row of strings it had three, the two outer rows tuned in unison to a diatonic scale and the central row supplying chromatic notes.

By the nineteenth century the triple harp was losing ground to the conventional single-strung pedal harp. Lady Llanover [58, 59], keen to support Welsh traditions in danger, set out to rescue it. She created scholarships for young harpists, commissioned Bassett Jones of Cardiff to make triple harps as prizes in eisteddfodau and competitions, and employed a resident harpist, John Wood Jones, at Llanover.

Roma like John Wood Jones had also helped keep the triple harp alive in Wales. He was said to descend from Abram Wood, who brought his family to Wales around 1730. He and other Roma became well known in north Wales for the excellence of their fiddle and harp playing. One of Abram's grandchildren, John Roberts, achieved fame as a triple harp player. Born in Llanrhaeadr-yng-Nghinmeirch [27] in 1816, he was a fluent Romany speaker. He served in the Royal Welch Fusiliers for nine years before marrying a Romany, Eleanor Wood Jones, and settling in Newtown to become a professional performer. He was taught to play by his uncle, Archelaus Wood, and later by Richard Roberts of Caernarfon. John Roberts won many competitions, including those at the Abergavenny eisteddfodau of 1842 and 1848 [59], combining Romany and Welsh traditions with ease. Many of his thirteen children were musicians. They often performed with him under the title The Roberts Family and The Cambrian Minstrels.

In 1885 Roberts was honoured at a ceremony on the shore of Llyn Geirionydd, organised by another John Roberts, a printer, bookseller and poet (his bardic name was Gwilym Cowlyd). The latter, indignant at the increasing anglicisation of the National Eisteddfod, had set up a rival festival, Arwest Glan Geirionydd, and a rival Gorsedd. In this remote spot, the supposed birthplace of the poet Taliesin, Gwilym Cowlyd gave Roberts the epithet 'Telynor Cymru' ('The Harpist of Wales').

This romanticised image of John Roberts appears in an oil portrait painted by an unknown artist in about 1890. The harpist is dressed in a long white robe with matching blue cloak and soft cap – possibly the bardic dress he wore to the Llyn Geirionydd ceremony. The robes, the flowing white beard and the solemn pose connect the picture with other nineteenth century imagined depictions of Welsh poets and musicians.

The triple harp tradition was passed on, notably through Nansi Richards, who maintained that she had been taught in part by Roma who stayed on the family farm in Pen-y-bont-fawr, Montgomeryshire.

Anonymous oil painting of John Roberts (Radnorshire Museum)

67

John Dillwyn Llewelyn and his camera
c.1853

The camera, said William Henry Fox Talbot, the English pioneer of photography, 'chronicles whatever it sees, and certainly would delineate a chimney-pot or a chimney-sweeper with the same impartiality as it would the Apollo of Belvedere'. Fox Talbot was related to the Talbots of Penrice, Gower, and often visited them. In 1833, when he began to experiment with fixing images on paper using what he called 'photogenic drawing', his cousin, Emma Talbot of Penrice, married John Dillwyn Llewelyn, the son of Lewis Weston Dillwyn [54].

In 1839 Llewelyn, who had studied chemistry at Oxford, began experimenting with photography techniques on his estate at Penlle'r-gaer just north of Swansea, together with Emma and their friend Calvert Richard Jones. Their initial interest was in the French daguerreotype process, published almost simultaneously with Talbot's invention. Calvert Jones used daguerreotype when he took the first known Welsh photograph, of Margam Castle, on 9 March 1841. But it was Talbot's technique that survived, and Jones and Llewelyn adopted a development of it, calotyping, that introduced a negative stage and allowed for multiple prints from a single exposure.

By 1852, when he was elected to the council of the Photographic Society of London, Llewelyn had turned his attention to the new 'wet collodion' process. This used glass rather than paper, and allowed sharper negatives and shorter exposure times. But the chemicals had to be coated onto the glass-plate immediately before exposure, while still damp, and had to be developed before they had time to dry out. For location photography this called for a portable darkroom, as in the image of Llewelyn posing beside his camera, developing tent behind him.

Llewelyn's invention of a falling shutter allowed him to pioneer instantaneous photographs, like one showing waves breaking on the beach of Caswell Bay in 1853. He won a silver medal for four such photographs at the Exposition Universelle in Paris in 1855. For the early Swansea photographers it was landscapes, pictures of their estates and possessions, and of their families, at home or on trips and holidays, that most appealed as subjects.

Like his father John Dillwyn Llewelyn had a wide interest in the sciences. In 1841 he sailed the first electrically-propelled boat in Britain on one of Penlle'r-gaer's lakes. An amateur botanist and landscape architect, he created one of the first orchid houses in Britain, and in 1851 built an observatory at Penlle'r-gaer as a gift to his eldest daughter, Thereza, also a photographer, where she would later help him take some of the earliest photographs of the moon.

Llewelyn's younger sister, Mary, was one of the first women photographers. Her small calotype salt prints, of flowers, animals, children and friends, tend to be more informal and intimate than her brother's. She used a smaller camera, which needed relatively short exposure times and was capable of taking more spontaneous pictures.

By 1860 the entire family had given up photography. Commercial photography was beginning, and the age of the pioneering amateur was over.

John Dillwyn Llewelyn's camera (National Waterfront Museum)

68 Hen Wlad Fy Nhadau
1856

As new nations emerged in Europe during the nineteenth century, national anthems were composed or adapted, as a conscious means of encouraging public identification with their communities. In Hungary, for example, the words of 'Himnusz', written by the poet Ferenc Kölcsey in 1823, were set to music by the composer Ferenc Erkel in 1844. The combination was quickly accepted as the unofficial national Hungarian anthem.

Wales followed a similar pattern. Words and music resulted from a collaboration, Evan James supplying the words and his son James the tune (which came first, words or music, is uncertain). James James was a harpist, entertaining people in the inns of his home town, Pontypridd. The manuscript of 'Hen Wlad Fy Nhadau' clearly notes him as the composer of the hymn-like melody, known as 'Glan Rhondda', and the date is given as January 1856. It had its first performance in the vestry of Capel Tabor, Maesteg in January or February 1856.

'Hen Wlad Fy Nhadau' has three stanzas, which include mention of patriotic feeling (*pleidiol wyf i'm gwlad*), military prowess (*gwrol ryfelwyr*), cultural accomplishment (*gwlad beirdd a chantorion*) and distinctive landscapes (*hen Gymru fynyddig, paradwys y bardd*). These are common elements in other national anthems. What is more distinctive is its emphasis on the continuance of the ancient Welsh language (*bydded i'r heniaith barhau*).

The anthem soon caught on. 'Glan Rhondda' was included in Owain Alaw's *Gems of Welsh Melody* (1860), which proved popular and rapidly spread awareness of 'Hen Wlad Fy Nhadau', as it was now known. Eisteddfod performances, like that by Robert Rees (Eos Morlais) in Bangor in 1874, were influential, and the anthem was increasingly sung at patriotic gatherings. It was sung by the crowd at the rugby international in 1905 between Wales and the New Zealand All Blacks, as a planned response to the Haka. This may have been the first ever singing of a national anthem at a major sporting event. By this time two life-size bronze statues commemorating its creators had been commissioned from William Goscombe John [23], after James James's death in 1902. They were finally unveiled in Ynysangharad Park, Pontypridd on 23 July 1930.

The anthem also began to be recorded – for the first time by Madge Breeze, who sang it on 11 March 1899 for a single-sided disc released by the Gramophone Company. A more recent recording is the guitar version played by Tich Gwilym in 1978 in imitation of Jimi Hendrix's 'The Star-Spangled Banner'. Whereas the lacerations and distortions of Hendrix's guitar might suggest an assault on the militant anthem of an imperial power, the character of the Welsh version is tamer and more respectful of the original.

When John Redwood, Secretary of State for Wales, was captured miming the words of 'Hen Wlad Fy Nhadau' at a Welsh Conservative party conference in 1993, he was widely derided. The episode symbolised for many in Wales the need for political devolution, and for an end to exclusive rule of their country by Westminster [98].

Monument to Evan and James James
(Ynysangharad Park, Pontypridd)

ni
Gwlad
Beirdd
a chantorion
enwogion
Dros
gollasant
eu gwaed
mor
yn
fûr

69 Cheap trip to Bangor
1859

In November 1855 'A Clwydian' wrote to the *North Wales Chronicle* protesting against a proposal to build a new railway line:

'The Vale of Clwyd is just now suffering from a severe attack of intermittent fever. I mean a railway fever... For a prospectus has actually been issued, capital, £60,000!! in ten pound shares, for a railway from Denbigh to Rhyl! And a more unpromising undertaking, as far as the shareholders, or a more useless one as far as the public are concerned, I think has never been suggested.'

The word 'fever' was already a cliché to describe the railway building passion that consumed Wales from the mid-1840s. Wealthy speculators invested their funds, and other people's money, in constructing new lines to serve the needs of industry and to transport passengers, including the new 'excursionists'. Sometimes plans were prepared and money gathered on the basis of zeal and hope rather than careful research. 'A Clwydian' objected that existing transport patterns did not suggest there was enough demand to justify a new railway. But in the next issue of the newspaper came a fierce attack on him – so fierce that the editor rebuked the author for his 'coarse and harsh expressions'.

The writer was Thomas Gee of Denbigh, a publisher and supporter of the new line. He claimed that 'a railway in 1855 is as essential to all progress as a good turnpike road was fifty years ago'. A railway 'diffuses union and prosperity wherever it extends'. Gee was a man of influence. In 1845 he had already begun publishing the magazine *Y Traethodydd* and would shortly launch the newspaper *Baner Cymru* (later *Baner ac Amserau Cymru*) and the ambitious encyclopedia *Y Gwyddoniadur Cymreig*. Through these organs he helped mould the new, dominant nonconformist voice of Wales: Welsh-speaking, nationalist, Liberal, devout, pro-temperance and anti-landlord – a powerful alternative to the Anglican, Conservative, landowning establishment. To T. Gwynn Jones [84] Gee was 'the one man who practically made modern Wales what it is politically'.

Resistance to the railway plans soon evaporated and Gee and his allies prevailed. They gained parliamentary approval and financial backers, and the Vale of Clwyd Railway was opened in October 1858. The contractors were David Davies of Llandinam and Thomas Savin of Oswestry. Davies [40] was at the start of his long career as a railway magnate and coal owner. His partner Savin was less successful. It was his bankruptcy in 1866 that allowed the Castle Hotel in Aberystwyth, which he had developed to house tourists arriving on his Cambrian Railway, to be bought cheaply by the new University College.

The Vale of Clwyd Railway was used for special cheap 'excursion' trains to take people from Denbigh, Rhuddlan and St Asaph to the seaside resorts, including Llandudno, Colwyn Bay and Bangor, that were growing up along the north Wales coast. These towns attracted visitors from northern England travelling along Robert Stephenson's Chester and Holyhead Railway, opened to Bangor in 1848. Occasionally tourism brought problems. In 1854 some visitors on a train from Birkenhead, fuelled by alcohol, ran riot in Bangor, fighting and vandalising property. No doubt those on the train from Denbigh on 14 September 1859 behaved impeccably, especially since the trip was arranged by the Calvinistic Methodist Association – possibly through Thomas Gee, the printer of the poster, who was an ordained Methodist minister.

VALE OF CLWYD RAILWAY.

CALVINISTIC METHODIST ASSOCIATION.

CHEAP TRIP

TO

BANGOR,

ON

Wednesday, September the 14th, 1859.

TIME & FARE TABLE FOR THE DOUBLE JOURNEY.

Denbigh	-	7. 0. a.m.	Fare	3s. 8d.
Trefnant	-	7. 10. -	-	3s. 6d.
St. Asaph	-	7. 26. -	-	3s. 3d.
Rhuddlan	-	7. 36. -	-	3s. 0d.
Rhyl -	-	8. 12. -		

Return.——Special Trains will leave **BANGOR** at 9. 15. p.m., by which Passengers will return.

September 9th, 1859.   DENBIGH, PRINTED BY THOMAS GEE.

70 Ophicleide
1860s

A common cultural feature of industrial working-class communities was the brass band. Like the choir the brass band brought non-professional musicians together to develop and share their skills. Instruments, mass-produced from about 1850, became cheap enough for local groups to buy through deferred payment schemes. Often employers supported bands, to encourage their workers to use their spare time constructively. But the first brass band to be founded in Wales was different: it was the personal possession of its founder, and it was in part professional.

Robert Thompson Crawshay **[60]** became manager of the Cyfarthfa ironworks in Merthyr Tydfil in 1839. In 1838 he had founded the Cyfarthfa Band, in part to play at social events such as concerts, balls and weddings held at Cyfarthfa Castle **[55]**. Most of the twenty or so players were ironworks employees and other local people, but others were professional musicians, some of them from circus bands. Many of their instruments survive. So do manuscript copies of over 100 examples of the band's repertoire, which included light waltzes, gallops and quadrilles, transcriptions of orchestral and operatic pieces, and occasional commissions. In the 1870s the Merthyr-born composer Joseph Parry wrote a 'Tydfil Concerto' for the band. The surviving brass instruments, such as bugles and trombones, are a mixture of older, keyed versions and later models with piston valves.

One of the band's instruments was the ophicleide, a keyed bass-baritone instrument patented in France in 1821. It had long, bent-back tubing and was played with a cupped mouthpiece, similar to that of a trombone. It was played in the classical orchestra as well as in brass bands. Crawshay hired a specialist musician to play the instrument. Sam Hughes, the son of a Staffordshire bricklayer, moved to Merthyr in the late 1850s and was given a job by Crawshay as a railway agent in the town. He remained with the band until about 1860, and later became professor of ophicleide at the Guildhall School of Music and the Royal Military School of Music. He died in poverty in 1898. His instrument predeceased him, killed off by the tuba (in orchestras) and euphonium (in brass bands).

The Cyfarthfa Band competed in the first national brass band contest at the Crystal Palace in 1860, winning two prizes. A writer in *Household Words* commented that the Band 'provided a rational and refined amusement for classes whose leisure time would otherwise probably be less creditably spent than learning or listening to music'. The Band survived the death of Robert Thompson Crawshay in 1879, but failed to maintain its standing. Crawshay had closed the Cyfarthfa ironworks in 1875, and refused to change his mind despite a mass protest by the workers, captured in a photograph, outside the castle two years later.

By now dozens of brass bands were active in industrial areas. Some promoted temperance, like the Cory Band (founded 1880) and the Tongwynlais Temperance Band (1888). Others had strong links with the labour movement and took part in marches and demonstrations.

Workers outside Cyfarthfa Castle
(Cyfarthfa Castle Museum and Art Gallery)

71 Three preaching giants
1869

Preaching was a public skill highly admired in Wales.
It was one of the main means by which the
nonconformist message was spread among the people.
The three acknowledged 'giants' of preaching were
John Elias, Christmas Evans and William Williams of
Wern. All three spent much of their time on the road,
attracting large, open air crowds and inflaming them by
the force of their rhetoric and character. They laid the
foundations for the nonconformist ascendancy in the
second half of the nineteenth century.

John Elias, the son of a weaver and farmer in
Aber-erch near Pwllheli, was self-taught. After a
spiritual crisis he joined the Calvinistic Methodists
and from his home in Llanfechell, Anglesey, began his
ceaseless preaching tours in 1796. He soon built a wide
reputation. In 1811 he was one of the first to be ordained
by the Methodists, in a ceremony at Bala that marked
their formal split from the Church of England. The
power of his preaching, over a period of thirty years and
more, had such an extraordinary effect on his followers
that he was called the 'Pope of Anglesey'. When he died
in 1841 10,000 people joined his funeral procession
near Beaumaris.

One of Elias's chief themes was sin. He saw it
all about him among the people, and never tired of
attacking it. At Rhuddlan in 1802 he found a fair being
held on the Sabbath, for the sale of farm implements
and the hiring of labourers. According to one account,
'when Elias arrived on the ground they were on the
point of engaging in their abominable transactions:
a great number had their hooks and scythes on their
arms and shoulders: there was the sound and noise
of harps and fiddles; the players were in liquor'. Elias

spoke from the steps of the inn and 'repeatedly thanked
the Lord that he did not suffer the earth to open and
swallow them alive into hell'. So powerful was his
speech that panic and remorse overcame his audience.
'A complete stop was put to the evil so rampant and
dreadful at Rhuddland'.

Elias's hardcore Calvinism and excoriation of
ungodly activity accelerated the movement towards the
sobriety, respectability and occasional censoriousness
that characterised nonconformist culture later in
the century. The growth of their denominations was
astonishing. By 1851 2,813 chapels had been built in
Wales, often in industrial areas ignored by the Church
of England, and usually employing the Welsh language.
Resolutely non-political at first, nonconformists began
to shape and dominate the public issues of the age,
including tithes, temperance and the disestablishment
of the Church. They acquired a taste for, and expertise
in, political engagement that would have been
anathema to Elias and his contemporaries.

Christmas Evans, too, was a charismatic preacher
with the Baptists **[62]**, while William Williams of Wern
was an Independent minister, with a lighter disposition
and an imaginative style. In 1869, long after their
deaths, the three 'giants' of Welsh nonconformity were
painted as a group by the artist William Williams (Ap
Caledfryn). He based his portraits on original pictures
– Christmas Evans, for example, had been painted
by Hugh Hughes **[65]**. His own portraits gained wide
circulation through print reproductions. John Thomas
[53] made money by selling photograph copies of
original paintings, and of 'preacher collections', such as
Enwogion y Pulpud Cymreig and *Y Tadau Ymneillduol*.

John Elias
o Fôn 1841
1774–1841

Tri Chedyrn Cymru
Y Parchedigion
—
Christmas Evans
1776–1838

W Williams
or Wern
1781–1840

72 Central star quilt
c.1875

In nineteenth century Wales women worked hard and for long hours, in the home or in the fields, but had few means of earning money for themselves. Domestic service in the households of well-off families was one way. Another was making and selling clothes and other textiles. A particular class of women cloth workers arose during the century: the quiltmakers.

Everyday quilts, made of wool or cotton enclosing woollen 'batting' or wadding, were bought to keep people warm in bed. More elaborate, decorative ones were kept as 'best', for example for the use of visitors, or were given as part of a marriage dowry. Most early quilts have failed to survive, but enough remain to show what a vibrant tradition existed, from about 1850 until the Second World War.

In earlier periods quilts were used to line armour, or were made by the daughters of wealthy families to demonstrate their accomplishment at sewing. But from the middle of the nineteenth century a cottage industry arose to supply less prosperous homes. Quilts were made and sold by professional workers, often spinsters or widows without other income. In rural areas some of them travelled from farm to farm, lodging with a family until the work was complete. The farm would store the rectangular wooden frame used to make the quilt, and the worker, perhaps assisted by an apprentice, would spend up to a fortnight producing quilts. An exceptionally dexterous and energetic quilter could finish two in one week.

The owner of the house normally selected and provided the fabric and filling. The filling was often wool, from scraps collected on hedgerows, or recycled blanket cloth. Local woollen flannel was the traditional material for the cover, but factory-produced cotton and satin-cotton were used for later quilts.

Most quilts were unsigned and their provenance is usually unknown, but this 'central star quilt', dating from about 1875, is known to be the work of an Aberdare quilter, Sara Lewis. She was a well-respected maker and her quilts were prized by their owners for their exceptional quality and originality of design. This example, measuring 209cm by 186cm, is made of flannel and wool and has a powerful geometric design. The front cover is built around the motif of an eight-pointed star, repeated with variations at each corner. The plan is completed with large rectangular blocks and bold zigzags. Like many distinctively Welsh quilts it features a variety of striking colours – red, black, dark blue, browns and greys. Some believe that the geometrical and colourful quilts made by the Amish community in the United States were influenced by those taken by Welsh emigrants to Pennsylvania.

The Welsh quilting industry declined after 1880, with the arrival of mass-produced bedding, and again after the First World War. It was revived through the action of the Rural Industries Bureau, set up in 1928 to stimulate craft industries in the economic depression (the Bureau also helped the Brynmawr Experiment [86]). Women received help to procure fabrics and filling, and their work, invariably of high quality, was sold through shops in Cardiff and London, often to hotels like Claridges and the Dorchester. Quilting was taught at Aberdare Technical College. This activity ceased with the Second World War, and quiltmaking, despite interest by new enthusiasts like Laura Ashley [94], became the smaller-scale and mainly non-commercial business it remains today.

73 Butter stamps
19th century

By 1851 more Welsh people worked in industry than on the land. For some this showed that Wales had become the world's first industrial nation. But farming was still the leading single source of employment (35% of employed men), and it continued to be important to the Welsh economy.

Making a living from the land was rarely easy, and profits were low. Farmers were affected by the vagaries of weather, the behaviour of landlords, changing markets and new technologies. In Carmarthenshire dairy farming was common, and after 1870 more land was given over to grazing and less to crops. Taking dairy products to centres of population by ship or road was laborious – the education commissioners of 1847 **[65]** interviewed a Carmarthen farmer who could not complete the journey to Swansea within twenty-four hours. There were also tolls to pay in both directions. But once Carmarthen was linked to the railway network in 1852 milk, butter and cheese could be transported to Swansea, and beyond, cheaply and quickly.

Most dairying was still small-scale. Butter and cheese were made on farms, using local herds. Butter making was a female job, often done by the farmer's wife, helped perhaps by a dairymaid. They milked cows in the field and stored the milk in shallow pans in a pantry. After they had collected enough cream they transferred it to a churn, which they agitated until lumps of butter formed within the buttermilk. Finally they added salt and formed the butter into pound or half-pound blocks, using pats and scales.

Then they printed the surface of each block with the mark of the individual farm, to indicate the source of the butter (there were originally no paper wrappers). The stamp was applied using a wooden tool, usually made from sycamore to avoid tainting the butter. Surviving prints show a large variety of shapes and designs – beehives, cows, thistles, leaves and flowers.

By 1911 only 12% of men in Wales were employed in farming, although the number of workers (96,000) had not declined drastically since 1851. Farmers were increasingly owners rather than tenants, as the great estates declined. Competitive pressures to produce cream, butter and cheese more efficiently led to the setting up of agricultural co-operatives and dairy factories in south-west Carmarthenshire. Later, as liquid milk became more profitable, milk lorries came to collect produce from individual farms. The establishment of the Milk Marketing Board in 1933 helped stabilise prices and the incomes of farmers.

Another engine of change was the growth of agricultural education. From the 1880s specialist schools taught the techniques of modern dairying, like the one in Nercwys, Flintshire (pictured). A cheese factory was set up in the village in 1919.

From 1850 many South Wales dairy workers, especially from Ceredigion, moved to London to keep cows and set up businesses supplying milk. In 1881 there were 240 cowkeepers in London with Welsh surnames, and even in the 1950s there were still 500 Welsh dairies in operation.

Nercwys dairy class (Flintshire Record Office)

74. Two Cardiganshire criminals
1900

Applications of the new technology of photography
[67] expanded rapidly. From 1850 prison and police authorities in Wales began to keep photographs of men and women convicted of crimes, as an aid to future identification.

The Cardiganshire Constabulary, set up in 1844 with 18 officers, followed suit. Between 1897 and 1933 it maintained its own photographic register of criminals, which records the minor offences committed in the county. Crimes, most of them related to poverty, included theft (including of 'rabbits', 'a ferret and nets', '32lbs of cattle hair'), robbery, burglary, vagrancy, assault and damage to property. The commonest punishments imposed by the magistrates at Quarter and Petty Sessions were hard labour and imprisonment.

Most of the criminals were working class men, typically termed 'labourers'. They wear poor clothes and often look older than the ages given in their written descriptions. The commonest crime of the women is theft, as in the case of Elizabeth Boswell. She is termed a 'gipsy' (Boswell was the name of a well-known Romany family). Roma were often the object of suspicion and prejudice, as people who failed, with some exceptions, to conform to the laws and norms of a settled lifestyle **[66]**. The *Cambrian News* reported her case: 'Elizabeth Boswell, hawker, Llandilo, was charged with having stolen a shilling by means of a trick from Alice Gater at the Pier Hotel, Aberystwyth, and also with having been drunk on the highway on Saturday evening, March 31st [1900]'. When arrested she was so drunk she had to be taken to the lock-up in a handcart. Her defence was hardly strong: 'I don't remember anything about it; if the girl says I took it she must be telling the truth.'

She was fined 20s and costs, or in default one month's hard labour, and was bound over on the charge of drunkenness.

Elizabeth's theft in the Pier Hotel was not her first offence. In 1897 she was sentenced in Carmarthen to nine months' imprisonment with hard labour for an assault on a deaf and dumb man, and in January 1899 she received two months' imprisonment for assault. In July 1899 Elizabeth Boswell and Matilda Price, described as 'pedlars', were convicted in Aberystwyth of stealing two sums of money from the house of Jane Ann Jones and Mary Anne Hughes in Llanbadarn Fawr. 'The prisoners entered their house', reported a newspaper, 'and picked up the money off the table, afterwards offering to tell their fortunes in exchange.' When asked to return the money 'they said they would kill them or "witchcraft" them'. The two were sent to prison for seven days with hard labour. In Carmarthen in July 1900 Elizabeth was charged under the name Emma Jones of committing grievous bodily harm against the landlady of the Red Lion Inn, Llandyfaelog. 'Her hat and shawl', a newspaper noticed, 'were of the bright hue commonly associated with the gipsies'.

Less is known about George Edwards of Tregaron. His desertion of his wife and child was possibly less of a concern to the magistrates than the additional cost to the Poor Law Union guardians of providing for them, either outdoors or, less likely, in the Aberystwyth workhouse. According to a report of 1894 the workhouse, on Penglais hill, was 'a cheerful-looking place, clean and well cared for'. Its inhabitants may have thought differently, and evidence from other workhouses **[51]** is not encouraging.

Elizabeth Boswell, Gipsy,
was fined 20/ and costs at
Aberystwyth for larceny at
the Pier Hotel Aberystwyth
31.3.00.

George Edwards, Tregaron,
Apprehended at Penybont
Radnor on the 14.5.00
for deserting his wife
and child and leaving
them chargeable to
Aberystwyth Union

James
melitia
sentence
H.L. for
Thomas
at Aber

John
Pen
seve
assa
and
to p

75 Mari Lwyd
Early 1900s

In 1852 a Baptist minister living in Blaina, William Roberts, published a book entitled *Crefydd yr Oesoedd Tywyll* ('The Religion of the Dark Ages'). Its subtitle was 'rituals, games and superstitions of the old world', and the author's aim was to draw his readers' attention to survivals of pagan and Catholic customs in Wales. He believed these should be rooted out as undesirable in contemporary society, and incompatible with its reformed morals. High on his list of pernicious superstitions was the Mari Lwyd, a wassailing tradition largely confined to south Wales ('Mari Lwyd' meant 'Grey Mare' or possibly 'Blessed Mary').

According to Roberts's account, the Mari Lwyd's journey began before Christmas, when young men went in search of the skull of a horse. To it they fixed a wooden jawbone, using a spring so that the mouth could be opened and snapped shut by the horse's operator. Then they attached multicolour ribbons, feathers and horsehair as a mane, and a wooden 'backbone' with a canvas sheet to hide the horseman below.

The Mari Lwyd and her human companions started their visits on Christmas Eve and would continue, sometimes for up to a month. They would approach a respectable house and sing a few verses, asking to be let in. The owner, refusing, made a witty response. Roberts gives examples of the verses sung. The Mari Lwyd begins (in translation),

> Well here we come,
> My blameless friends,
> We ask your permission – to sing.

> Six men of good will,
> The salt of the earth,

To sing in truth – for beer.

Usually, after a lengthy verse dialogue, the horse was the winner and was admitted with its entourage. Inside, the horse pursued the women of the house, breathing, sniffing, biting and whinnying. The other visitors danced and sang to a crwth **[46]**, before sitting down to eat and drink ale. They wished their hosts a prosperous new year before rounding up the Mari Lwyd and moving on to the next house to begin again.

To Roberts the Mari Lwyd tradition was a symptom of the sad persistence of Catholicism in Wales. He dismissed a rival theory that Mari Lwyd was a famous warrior princess from pre-Christian times. Others since have argued for a Dark Ages origin, but there is no written evidence for the Mari Lwyd earlier than 1800.

At the end of his discussion Roberts hopes for 'this foolishness, and all similar follies, to have no place anywhere except in the museum of an historian or antiquary'. The editor of the newspaper *Seren Cymru* agreed, warning that the custom was as rampant as ever in Cwmaman, where 'a swarm of idlers dressed more like fiends from the bottomless pit than rational people' terrified householders.

Roberts's is one of the most detailed early accounts of the Mari Lwyd. Its publication may have had the opposite effect to the one intended, since there is evidence of several revivals of the custom. The Mari Lwyd opposite came from Llangynwyd in the early 1900s, and the custom is still alive in the village today. In 2012 a project to promote the Mari Lwyd made available a cardboard flat-pack kit, to 'address the barrier of obtaining a horse's head'.

76 The Great Strike at Penrhyn
1900

By 1899 over 2,500 men were employed at the Penrhyn slate quarry owned by Lord Penrhyn [52]. North Wales now produced over 90% of the slate quarried in Britain, and Penrhyn's quarry was the world's largest.

George Sholto Gordon Douglas-Pennant, 2nd Baron Penrhyn, educated at Eton and Oxford, was an Anglican Tory of immense wealth. In 1886 he inherited his father's estates, over 72,000 acres in Wales alone, and the quarry, which earned him over £100,000 a year. His interests included racing horses, hunting and fishing. The quarrymen, who had little formal education but were by no means uncultured, were overwhelmingly Welsh-speaking, nonconformist and radical in politics. Their work was hard, dangerous and poorly paid, but the skilled slate workers – rockmen, splitters and dressers – were intensely proud of their craft.

If owner and workers had little in common culturally, the industrial gulf between them was still wider. Lord Penrhyn was willing to buy allegiance through paternalism, but insisted that he held ultimate power to direct the quarry and its workforce. The workers treasured the traditional system of 'bargain', a method of organising work and payments that was partly under their control. A pay dispute in 1874 led to the foundation of the North Wales Quarrymen's Union. The union seldom represented much more than half of the Penrhyn Quarry workers, but it was anathema to Penrhyn. He was intent on breaking its collective strength and the bargain system.

In 1896-7 a long strike about recognition of the union poisoned relations. On 5 November 1900 the men walked out, angered by the suspension of some workers and a law case brought against others. On 6 November Penrhyn's manager, E.A. Young, put up posters to say that all the strikers were suspended from work for two weeks. Young, a London accountant, was intransigent and contemptuous of the workers. 'These Welshmen', he wrote, 'are so ignorant and so childish that there is no arguing with them.' On 22 November, after another dispute about the letting of bargains, the entire workforce went on strike and left the quarry, which Penrhyn then closed down. Most never returned.

Many strikers migrated to south Wales to find work in the collieries. The rest held demonstrations, gathered support and assistance, and attempted to negotiate a resolution. They exerted social control to dissuade men from returning to employment, especially when Penrhyn reopened the quarry in June 1901. Blacklegs who broke the strike were hooted, threatened and barred from pubs, shops and chapels. They were known as *cynffonwyr*, 'creatures with tails – taking the form of men, but not men', in the words of one striker. Strikers displayed posters in their house windows saying, '*Nid oes bradwr yn y tŷ hwn*' ('No scab here').

Penrhyn refused all attempts at arbitration. By November 1903 the union was exhausted. Defeated, men not on Young's blacklist returned to work. The quarry, and the slate industry, never recovered, as competition increased and demand for slate fell. The bitterness caused by the long dispute lingered for decades.

Window poster (Gwynedd Archive Services)

PENRHYN QUARRY.

NOTICE.

Inasmuch as a number of the Penrhyn Quarry Employees has during the last fortnight actively participated in certain acts of violence and intimidation against some of their fellow-workmen and officials, and to-day nearly all the Employees have left their work without leave, Notice is hereby given that such Employees are suspended for 14 days.

E. A. YOUNG

PORT PENRHYN,
Bangor, November 6th, 1900.

Chwarel y Penrhyn.

RHYBUDD.

Yn gymaint ag i nifer o weithwyr Chwarel y Penrhyn yn ystod y pythefnos diweddaf gymeryd rhan weithredol mewn ymosodiadau o greulondeb a bygythiadau yn erbyn rhai o'u cyd-weithwyr a swyddogion, ac heddyw i agos yr oll o'r gweithwyr adael eu gwaith heb ganiatad, rhoddir Rhybudd drwy hyn fod y cyfryw weithwyr yn cael eu hatal am bedwar-diwrnod-ar-ddeg.

E. A. YOUNG

PORT PENRHYN,
Bangor, Tachwedd 6ed, 1900.

In the 1900 general election a Scottish trade union leader, 'the greatest agitator of his day', was elected to represent Merthyr Tydfil, to the surprise of almost everyone, including himself. James Keir Hardie was the first Labour MP to be elected to parliament.

Eight months earlier Keir Hardie and others had set up the Labour Representation Committee, renamed the Labour Party in 1906, to bring together trade unions with political parties and societies, notably the Independent Labour Party (ILP), with the aim of gaining direct representation in parliament for working people.

The LRC did not have long to wait. In September 1900 the Conservative government called a snap general election, to exploit jingoistic feeling about the South African war and splits over the war within the Liberal Party. In Merthyr the local branch of the ILP, which had nearly 300 members, decided to nominate a candidate. Though the miners' leaders preferred a local man, Keir Hardie won the nomination. The Conservative Party failed to put up a candidate, and in the contest for the two seats available in the constituency Keir Hardie faced two sitting Liberal MPs, Pritchard Morgan and D.A. Thomas. These two men detested each other so much – Morgan was an aggressive imperialist, Thomas an opponent of the war – that Keir Hardie gathered Thomas's endorsement and the votes of many Liberal supporters.

Keir Hardie had other advantages. He was well known in south Wales. 'We are no strangers to one another', he wrote to the electors. 'I was among you endeavouring to cheer, encourage and strengthen you in the dark days of your recent great industrial struggle',

referring to the miners' strike and lockout of 1898 [80]. He was helped by an energetic team of organisers, members of a new generation of ILP and trade union activists who had lost faith in the belief that the cause of workers could best be advanced through the Liberal Party.

Keir Hardie polled 5,745 votes, taking one of the seats at the expense of Morgan, who blamed Thomas's treachery for 'ousting me from the seat which I have occupied for the last twelve years'. For many years the Labour Party needed to cooperate tactically with sections of the Liberal Party until it was strong enough to work on its own. Six Labour candidates were nominated in 1900, but Keir Hardie was one of only two to be elected. At the next general election in 1906, when he was re-elected, the party gained 29 MPs, thanks to a pact with the Liberals. By now the labour movement was beginning to organise effectively. The ILP was stronger, an LRC branch had been set up in Merthyr in 1903, the miners' leaders had abandoned their hostility, and Labour candidates were being elected to local government boards. The House of Lords' ruling in the Taff Vale case that employers could sue trade unions for striking, so threatening the financial future of unions, acted as a recruiting spur for the movement. By 1903, according to Keir Hardie in a speech in Pontypridd, 'Wales had become the cockpit in which great questions affecting labour were being fought out'. He was re-elected as one of the two MPs for Merthyr in both the elections of 1910. But his later opposition to the First World War [84] cost him support and his own health, and he died in September 1915.

VOTE FOR HARDIE,

THE LABOUR CANDIDATE.

Vote for HARDIE

AND THE FOLLOWING PROGRAMME:

1. — Temperance Reform.
2. — Disestablishment.
3. — Old Age Pensions.
4. — Eight Hours for Miners and Railwaymen.
5. — Adult Suffrage.
6. — Abolition of the House of Lords.
7. — Home Rule all Round.
8. — Railway Nationalization.
9. — Taxation of Land Values and Royalties.
10. — Better and Brighter Homes for the People
11. — Extension of the Compensation Act
12. — Extension of the Conciliation and Arbitration Acts.

REMEMBER:

The rich and powerful can protect themselves: Parliaments exist to make laws for the workers and the poor.

Printed and Published by John P. Lewis &c High Street, Merthyr

78 Early Carmarthenshire motor car
c.1904

In November 1896 Lord Tredegar's Show was held at Newport. Charles D. Phillips, the owner of the Emlyn Engineering Works in the town, had a stand there. 'Its most attractive feature', said a newspaper report, 'was the horseless carriage, one of Benz's system, and a car that arrived amongst the first lot, which journeyed from London to Brighton on Saturday ... Mr Phillips had great difficulty and expense in bringing it to the show, but he did not want *Newport* to be behind. He is paying every attention to this new thing, and can give advice to anyone requiring it, and he wants to keep what he believes an immense industry in the district if possible.'

This may have been the first appearance of a motor car in Wales. Soon, as some of the restrictions on driving motor vehicles on public roads were lifted, cars and vans began to be seen on roads. But until mass production reduced their price cars tended to be bought only by wealthy enthusiasts. In 1904 only 8,465 cars were registered in Britain. One early purchaser was Isaac Hayley, the owner of Glanbrân mansion near Llandovery. Around 1904, when car registration was introduced, he bought a motor with the registration plate 'UM7'. It was a Mercedes, or possibly a copy. A keen amateur photographer, he probably took the picture himself, recruiting local people to pose for it. A fashionably dressed lady sits in the back, while three country people wrapped in flannels occupy the other seats. 'UM7' was driven, slowly and uncomfortably on its solid tyres, around the county's roads. Another Hayley photograph shows it outside a cottage in Rhandirmwyn, the first time, apparently, a motor car had been seen there. This may not have been

Hayley's only car. His great niece recalled a chauffeur driving him to Llandovery in a Daimler.

By 1910 cars were common enough that garages selling and servicing them began to appear. In the Crown Garage, Llandovery T. Roberts & Sons sold Ford cars coming off the new, fast production lines. Garages often developed from the bicycle shops that had responded to the enthusiasm for cycling in the 1890s. In Llandrindod Wells Tom Norton opened his cycle shop in the High Street in 1898, and built a large new garage in 1911, naming it the 'Palace of Sport' (later it was known as the 'Automobile Palace'). From 1899 the retired champion cyclist George Ace sold cars from his bicycle shop in Tenby.

Charles Phillips's hopes for an 'immense' Welsh motor industry went unfulfilled **[91]**. But another Monmouthshire figure, Charles Rolls, became a pioneer of motor engineering. In 1904 he showed in Paris the first Rolls-Royce car, designed in partnership with his friend Henry Royce. In 1905, next to the family home, The Hendre, near Monmouth, his father built for him an extravagantly equipped motor-house or car workshop, that still survives today.

Isaac Hayley lived in Glanbrân until his death in 1929. By this time cars had ceased to be the preserve of the rich. In 1914 over 132,000 cars were registered in Britain; in 1929 there were 981,000. The spread of car ownership reflected an economic shift towards the new middle class and away from the traditional holders of wealth. Glanbrân, already in poor condition, was sold and dismantled in 1930. Nothing remains of the house and its estate.

79 Evan Roberts mug
c.1905

Evan Roberts was a young ex-coal miner from Loughor, training for the Methodist ministry. In November 1904, at Blaenannerch near Cardigan, he was overcome by an intense vision. 'The salvation of souls weighed heavily on me. I felt on fire for going through the whole of Wales to tell the people about the Saviour'. Beginning in Loughor, he made seven tours, mainly in south Wales, speaking twice a day. Thousands flocked to his ecstatic meetings, singing and praying for hours. Pubs closed, sports grounds and theatres were abandoned, crime declined and the chapels were filled.

That, at least, is the traditional story of the 1904-5 Welsh religious revival. The truth is more complex. 'Revivals' were common in Wales. The last national example had been in 1858-9, but at least six local revivals had occurred since. In Cardiganshire a vigorous campaign was under way, led by Joseph Jenkins, John Thickens and Seth Joshua. Other revivalists were active in north Wales. People were already receptive to Roberts's message before he arrived.

It was the press that assigned Roberts the leading role in the revival. By 1900 newspapers reached a mass audience, and their owners were conscious of their ability to affect public opinion. Reporters attended Roberts's earliest meetings in Loughor:

'The proceedings commenced at seven o'clock, and they lasted without a break until 4.30 o'clock on Friday morning. During the whole of this time the congregation were under the influence of deep religious fervour and exaltation ... [Roberts] walked up and down the aisles, open Bible in hand, exhorting one, encouraging another, and kneeling with a third to implore a blessing from the throne of grace. People dropped as if struck. A young woman rose to give out a hymn which was sung with deep earnestness. While it was being sung several people dropped down in their seats ... and commenced crying for pardon.'

The *Western Mail* devoted many columns each day to Roberts, with eyewitness reports, biographies, interviews, letters and pictures. Headlines included 'Women fainting and men weeping' and 'An atheist burns his books'. Roberts was an instant celebrity. His image was applied to household mugs, and his words to wax cylinders (one was restored in 2004, reviving his voice).

The press focus on Roberts may have harmed his cause. Some ministers attacked his campaign as 'a sham revival, a mockery, a blasphemous travesty of the real thing'. His emotionalism, they claimed, exploited vulnerable young women, and he lacked respect for chapel authorities. Roberts also showed signs of mental instability; a complete breakdown in early 1906 signalled the end of his campaign.

The revival's origins have been much debated. Though chapel membership had never been higher, many nonconformists feared that members attended out of habit, not conviction, and that secularists and socialists were undermining Christian faith. The passion and energy of the early Methodists needed to be regained.

The revival stimulated a temporary growth in chapel membership, but could not halt the long decline of religious practice and belief in Wales.

Wax cylinder of Evan Roberts's voice (National Library of Wales)

80 Holing the coal
c.1905

By 1900 coal had transformed Wales. It was in high demand to power steam engines at land and sea, both at home and overseas: 39.3m tons of coal were mined in south Wales in 1900. In 1851 only about 2,000 people lived in the pre-industrial Rhondda valleys; there were over 113,000 in 1901. Most adult men were employed in the seventy or more collieries of the Rhondda, where a continuous ribbon of towns and villages developed. Outside the coalfield, Cardiff, Swansea and later Barry grew as coal-exporting ports. Rural Wales supplied labour to the industry, and all Wales benefited to an extent from the wealth coal created.

Some mines employed over 1,000 workers each and were owned by large combines, like David Davies's Ocean Coal Company. But it was in one of the many smaller pits that William E. Jones, a Pontypool miner's 13-year-old son, took pioneering photographs of miners underground. He carried a half-plate camera and tripod. For lighting he used a flash pan and magnesium, avoiding areas prone to explosive gases.

The miner is working in a 'stall', at the end of a 'side heading' off the main tunnel in the Plas y Coed mine near Pontypool. Beside a timber roof support and with the aid of a bare candle, he uses his mandrel or one-sided pick to hack a horizontal layer of coal away at the base of the seam, and make a vertical cut up the seam's full height. This procedure, known as 'holing the coal', allowed the rest of the coal to be removed by wedging, hammering or

blasting. When interviewed in 1974, Jones recognised the miner as a man who competed with his father to gain the best stall and the 'dram' or small truck used to collect and move the coal.

The work was cramped, dark and very dangerous. Accidents were common and disasters almost annual. Lung diseases were prevalent. Working with only candles for light could lead to nystagmus, an involuntary oscillation of the eyeball.

William Jones took his photographs for his father, Jabez Jones, an active member of the South Wales Miners' Federation. Jabez often gave talks about the need to improve the pay and working conditions of miners. His lantern slides showed his son's vivid photographs, developed and prepared at home. William recalled, 'we had an eighteen-foot frame with a fifteen-foot sheet fixed to it and the carbide for making the gas in the lantern'. Jabez and his wife had eight children: 'it was all Miners' Federation and children in those days'.

The Federation had been founded in 1898 after a bitter lockout by the employers. It fought for, and gained, the end of the sliding scale, which linked miners' pay to the price of coal, and soon became a strong voice for the miners' cause. The Independent Labour Party, of which Jabez was also a member, gained support after the strike, paving the way for the representation of labour in Parliament [77].

Gordon's map of the South Wales coalfield
(National Library of Wales)

81 Billy Meredith's cap
1910

Football and rugby, the two main organised sports in Wales, grew out of the industrial society developing in south and north-east Wales. For working class players and spectators sport was a release from the power and discipline of industrial production.

The roots of Welsh football lay in the north-east. The Football Association of Wales, the dream of a local solicitor, Llewelyn Kenrick, arose from a meeting in the Wynnstay Arms, Wrexham in February 1876, aimed at organising an international match against Scotland. The match was played in Glasgow in March. Though Wales lost, and lost again in a return match in Wrexham in 1877, the seeds were sown for a flourishing football culture in the Wrexham and Ruabon area. By 1900 football had spread to south Wales and attracted large crowds.

The first star of the game in Wales – and one of the greatest ever – was Billy Meredith. He was born near Chirk in 1874. His father worked in the Black Park colliery, one of the oldest in north Wales, and at the age of twelve Billy followed him, working pit ponies, pushing wheeled trucks and firing boilers. He soon showed signs of being a promising footballer, and at fifteen was in the Chirk reserves team. By nineteen he was playing for Northwich Victoria in the Football League's second division. In September 1894 he signed as a professional player with Manchester City. On his club debut he finished work in the pit on Friday, caught an overnight train to Newcastle to play in the match, and returned to Chirk for his Sunday night shift. He finally gave up his pit job in January 1895.

Playing on the right wing, Meredith won a reputation for his skill at ball control and swift, accurate passing. He was a prolific goal scorer. Some of his artistry is clear in surviving film of the 1910 Wales v England international in Wrexham. His preparation for games was rigorous. He prided himself on his fitness, and neither smoked nor drank alcohol. His trademark habit was to suck on a toothpick throughout matches. He captained the Manchester City side which gained promotion and won the FA Cup in 1904.

In 1905 the Football Association found Meredith guilty of trying to fix the result of a game, and he was banned from playing for eighteen months. But he soon resumed his career, now with Manchester United, and continued playing football until 1924, when he was almost fifty years old. He appeared for Wales 48 times, a record for his period, and scored 11 goals. On 5 March 1910 he won a cap – 'winning a cap' meant receiving a real cap – for playing in the game against Scotland at Kilmarnock. 'W. Meredith, the famous winger', reported a newspaper, 'to-day played his thirty-first international for "gallant little Wales"'. Despite their gallantry the Welsh lost the match 1-0. 'It was by Meredith that most of the Welsh attacks were initiated and as he seldom failed to get the ball well into the goal he was a constant source of danger.'

Billy Meredith was a determined man off the pitch, defending fiercely the professional status of his fellow footballers. In 1907 he helped establish the Players' Union, chairing its first meeting in Manchester. The Union campaigned to get rid of the maximum wage and the restriction on players moving between clubs.

82 Two suffragette dolls
c.1910

Democracy was late in coming to Britain. Despite Reform Acts in 1832, 1867 and 1884, and the efforts of the Chartists and their successors, well over half the population was still ineligible to vote in elections at the end of the nineteenth century. That included over 40% of men, and all women.

Pressure to enfranchise women grew in the second half of the nineteenth century. John Stuart Mill and others argued the cause, and bills were presented to Parliament regularly after 1870. But resistance was strong. Women were dismissed as too weak or irrational or otherwise unqualified to deserve the vote.

Women began to organise themselves, locally and nationally, to demand change. The National Union of Women's Suffrage Societies, established in 1897, relied on constitutional means like lobbying Parliament, public meetings, petitioning and publicity. Emmeline and Christabel Pankhurst set up their own group, the Women's Social and Political Union, which later used more militant means. 'Suffragettes' chained themselves to railings, set fire to property and disrupted public meetings.

Welsh women were at the forefront of these movements. The country's first women's suffrage organisation, set up in Llandudno in January 1907, was followed rapidly by over thirty others. By 1912 the Cardiff and District Women's Suffrage Society was the largest local group outside London. Its co-founder was Millicent Mackenzie, professor of education at Cardiff and later the only woman candidate in Wales in the 1918 general election. A militant but non-violent splinter group of the WSPU, the Women's Freedom League, had a particularly strong branch in Swansea, founded in 1909 and led by Emily Phipps.

One of the movement's more radical leaders was the businesswoman Margaret Haig Mackworth, later Lady Rhondda, who set up the Newport branch of the WSPU. In 1913 she received a prison sentence for setting fire to letters in a postbox in Newport. She was released after going on hunger strike, a common suffragette tactic. Lloyd George, a particular target of the suffragettes, was hounded by campaigners on many occasions when he spoke in Wales.

'Miss Flora Copper' reflects faithfully the typical campaigner. She is a middle class, well-educated woman, with a determined attitude. She wears the suffragette colours of purple, white and green. The doll may have been sold at a fair organised to promote the franchise cause – or it may have had a satirical, punning intent ('floor a copper').

The second doll is certainly intended to prompt derision or contempt. Her head is a ping pong ball, her face wears a grimace, and her clothes have seen better days. Worse, pins have been stuck into her head and body, as if in a voodoo rite. This is an anti-suffrage doll. It testifies to the strength of feeling among those opposed to the franchise, even among women themselves. They had their own organisation, the Women's National Anti-Suffrage League, founded in 1908, which by 1910 had branches in Cardiff, Newport and north Wales. In 1910, however, the league was obliged to merge with the Men's National League for Opposing Women's Franchise.

In 1918, at the end of the First World War, women finally gained the right to vote in general elections. Even then, those under 30 years of age were excluded, and it was not until 1928 that most women and men aged 21 and over could vote.

83 Butetown residents
c.1918

Before the First World War most south Wales coal was exported. By 1907, when the Alexandra Dock opened, Cardiff was the world's largest coal exporting port, shipping nine million tons a year. Commercial buildings grew up around the port – banks, shipping offices and the Coal Exchange, opened in 1883. Houses were needed for the seamen, dockers and other workers, and a new, planned district arose – Butetown, named after the port's owner, the 2nd Marquis of Bute.

Butetown, a dense grid of terraced streets centred on Loudon Square, housed a mix of people from the British Empire and beyond. From Ireland and Norway, Somalia and Yemen, the West Indies, Spain, Italy, and elsewhere, they built a community where languages, religions and cultures lived closely together. Around 700 non-white people were said to live in Cardiff in 1914.

Many more arrived during the First World War – according to one estimate, 1,000 black Cardiff seamen lost their lives in the conflict. By 1919 between 1,000 and 2,000 people of Arab descent lived in the city, most demobilised and many out of work. Soon after the war an unknown photographer captured a group of Butetown people about to leave on an excursion. In the foreground stand six men, mainly black, wearing smart suits and hats. Some may be musicians (one holds a guitar). Women and children, in their best dresses and hats, sit behind in a horse-drawn brake.

As unemployment and depression took hold after the war, tensions rose in the docks. British-born workers blamed overseas seamen for benefiting from the war, and accused them of undercutting rates of pay and competing for scarce housing. In June 1919 discontent turned into racial violence. A crowd of white men came across a brake – probably of the type shown in the photograph – containing black men and their white wives returning from an excursion. Hostility to the cross-racial relationships of the black men and their perceived affluence spilled over into conflict, which left three men dead and dozens injured.

A unique account survives of the fighting, written by a young Somali newly arrived in Butetown, Ibrahim Ismaa'il: 'In Millicent Street, the fight started at about 7:30pm and lasted a fairly long time. Seven or eight Warsangeli defended the house and most of them got badly wounded. Some of the white people also received wounds. In the end, the whites took possession of the first floor, soaked it with paraffin oil and set it alight. The Somalis managed to keep up the fight until the police arrived. One of them was left for dead in the front room and was later carried to the hospital where he recovered; some escaped through a neighbouring house and came to tell us the story of what had happened, the others gave themselves up to the police, and we did not see them for a long time. Most of our countrymen were now in prison, on remand. When their case came before the magistrates, it was recognised that they had acted in self-defence, and they were set free.'

Butetown later attracted competing mythologies. Some feared Tiger Bay, to use the title of the 1959 film, as a sink of crime, violence and vice, and gave it a wide berth. For romantic progressives Butetown came to stand for the warmth of a multiracial community living in harmony.

84. Tabernacl war memorial
1921

Most Welsh people, even if they did not welcome the Great War when it began in August 1914, soon became caught up in the passion for conflict. They had a duty, said David Lloyd George in a speech to London Welshmen in September, to help 'little Belgium' after its invasion by Germany, 'the road-hog of Europe'. He called for sacrifice, 'in the form of the glory and thrill of a great movement for liberty' – 'the great pinnacle of sacrifice pointing like a rugged finger to Heaven'. As a focus for Welsh military pride he urged the establishment of a new Welsh Regiment.

In Aberystwyth, a centre for billeting troops and for Belgian refugees, men signed up to fight, urged on by trade unions, politicians, academics and chapel preachers as well as by government. Objectors to war were treated with contempt and worse. The poet T. Gwynn Jones, a lecturer in the University College, kept a bitter, disillusioned diary recording the erosion of civilised values as war fever took hold. 'I cannot stand the attitude of the preachers and the churches', he wrote. 'They go into the pulpits to bless war.' He worshipped in Tabernacl, a Calvinistic Methodist chapel. 'One evening [in September 1915] when the Rev. R.J. Rees officiated, I failed to put up with it any longer, & left the building when they were singing after the introductory prayer, which was no better than a barbarian's appeal to the god of his tribe.' Jones also described the 'hunt for aliens', including the hounding of Hermann Ethé, a German-born professor in the

Are YOU in this?

college since 1875, who was forced to flee Aberystwyth in October 1914 by a threatening mob.

By the end of the war in November 1918 over 1,100 Cardiganshire men had been killed. In 1921 the Tabernacl elders asked an Italian sculptor, Mario Rutelli, to design a bronze memorial to fourteen members who had died. Most were privates on the Western Front. A graceful winged angel plants a foot on a globe inscribed with the names of the men killed. Dressed in a tunic, garlanded and bearing palm leaves, he may symbolise Victory, but his mood is elegiac, not triumphal.

Two years later, to commemorate the 111 men from Aberystwyth who died in the War, Rutelli completed a more grandiloquent and conventional memorial. Here on Castle Point Lloyd George's 'great pinnacle of Sacrifice pointing like a rugged finger to Heaven' is realised in stone and bronze. At its top is a winged female Victory, at its foot a naked woman emerging from the tangle of war.

The war changed Wales. Nationalisation of industries essential to the war, like coal and the railways, pointed to the possibilities of state action in peacetime. The labour movement gathered strength. Women were attracted into work vacated by absent men, especially after conscription was introduced in March 1916. They found themselves in new, better paid jobs, in offices, shops, factories and fields (Cardiganshire, it was claimed, had the largest Women's Land Army in Britain).

World War 1 recruitment poster (National Library of Wales)

85 Pembroke Dock Cooperative Society store

c.1922

In the nineteenth century shops multiplied, and the shopping experience became more varied. Cardiff's distinctive arcades were developed from 1858, in Newtown the mail order store was pioneered [94], and department stores opened in larger towns from the 1870s. And a new kind of shop arose – the co-operative store, whose customers enjoyed a share in its ownership and profits.

The co-operative model grew from the ideas and practice of Robert Owen, born in Newtown in 1771. After a basic education he worked in drapers' shops in London and Manchester before finding success in the cotton industry. As manager of the New Lanark mill on the river Clyde he put into practice his ideas about improving the conditions, education and pay of the mill workers. In 1813 he opened a store, selling good quality goods at reasonable prices, with profits being used for workers' education. His aim was for workers to 'exchange their poverty for wealth, their ignorance for knowledge, their anger for kindness, their divisions for union'.

Owen died in 1858 and was buried in Newtown, but already others had taken up his ideas. From the 1840s co-operative shops opened in north-west England and elsewhere, owned and democratically run by their members, who received regular dividends. The movement developed slowly in Wales, but from the late 1880s co-operative societies operated in many towns. Co-operators aimed to offer members a coherent, alternative 'cradle to grave' service. As well as shops they offered bakeries, banks and other facilities, and organised social and community activities like choirs, libraries and education classes.

The Pembroke Dock Co-operative Society was founded in 1888. Joseph John convened a meeting of 38 local people to propose opening a co-operative shop. The response was encouraging, a committee was formed to organise 'a Society on co-operative principles, on the Rochdale system', and subscribers were recruited. The first shop operated from Joseph John's front room, before rooms were rented at 41 Bush Street. Soon a bakery opened in Pembroke Street, and a donkey and cart and 'boy' were employed to make home deliveries. In 1893, against opposition from other traders, the society opened a new building on three floors in Albion Square; a bakery and warehouse were soon added.

The shop interior, photographed in the early 1920s, is packed with hardware and other goods, arrayed on shelves and stands and hanging from the ceiling. Much of the produce was supplied to the society by the Co-operative Wholesale Society. Seven white-coated staff stand ready to help customers. A large poster advertises the 'Chocolate Club', a national initiative organised by the Women's Co-operative Guild to sell the Co-op's Lutonia chocolate. Each week customers contributed a small sum to ensure that a box of chocolates could be shared with relatives at Christmas.

The Pembroke Dock Society, which developed branches in Pembroke, Neyland, Goodwick and Milford Haven, adapted to changing shopping patterns, introducing self-service and opening a superstore in Gordon Street in the 1970s. The last Co-op in the town, however, closed in 2005.

Life mask of Robert Owen (Robert Owen Museum)

86 Tredegar Medical Aid Society window
1920s

In the early 1870s a Health and Education Fund was organised in Tredegar, overseen by a joint employers' and workers' committee. Under the scheme workers of the Tredegar Iron and Coal Company paid regular subscriptions at the rate of 1¾d in the pound. In return the fund employed a doctor to provide free medical care and sickness pay. By the 1880s the committee had become the Tredegar Medical Aid Society, and a decade later its membership had grown to embrace other local industries.

In 1904 the society opened the Tredegar Park Cottage Hospital, on land donated by Lord Tredegar. A separate Hospital Management Committee was set up to run the new facility. In 1907 a women's and children's ward was opened, and in 1914 a new wing was built.

From 1915 until his death in 1933 the Medical Aid Society's energetic and respected secretary was Walter Conway, an ex-miner and Independent Labour Party activist. In 1924 Aneurin Bevan [91], one of Conway's protégés and a miners' agent, joined the Hospital Management Committee. He became its chair in 1929, in the year he was elected to Parliament for the first time. Conway, Bevan and others worked to wrest control of the committee from the company's influence, and to encourage the society towards providing a universal service to the whole community. The Tredegar scheme became the most comprehensive of the medical societies in Wales. In the 1920s it employed five doctors, a surgeon, two pharmacists, a physiotherapist, a dentist and a district nurse. By 1946 95% of Tredegar's population was eligible for treatment.

The novelist A.J. Cronin worked for three years in the early 1920s as a doctor for the Tredegar Society. In *The Citadel* (1937), where Cronin appears as Dr Andrew Manson and Tredegar as 'Aberalaw', Manson's resentment at the democratic oversight of doctors is obvious: 'It was a wonderful ideal, this group of working men controlling the medical services of the community for the benefit of their fellow workers. But it was only an ideal. They were too biased, too unintelligent ever to administer such a scheme progressively'. In his autobiography Cronin called the Tredegar scheme 'a malingerer's and hypochondriac's paradise'.

During the 1920s and 1930s colliery closures and increasing unemployment reduced the society's income while increasing demand on its services. In 1926, the year of the General Strike and miners' lockout, expenditure exceeded income by £2,741. The management committee reported that 'the year has been one of great difficulty'. In 1927 it felt obliged to launch a fundraising campaign, including a plea to shopkeepers encouraging their customers to donate silver paper and tinfoil.

By August 1945 Aneurin Bevan was Minister of Health in the new Labour government. His first priority was setting up the new National Health Service, which came into being on 5 July 1948. Bevan acknowledged that the subscription-based health service developed at Tredegar had succeeded in giving workers medical care that was free when they needed it. But local schemes, however good, had weaknesses. Their unplanned nature and small scale created 'a patch-quilt of local paternalisms', and they relied on private and charitable income. In April 1946 he said in the House of Commons, 'I believe it is repugnant to a civilised community for hospitals to have to rely upon private charity. I believe we ought to have left hospital flag days behind.'

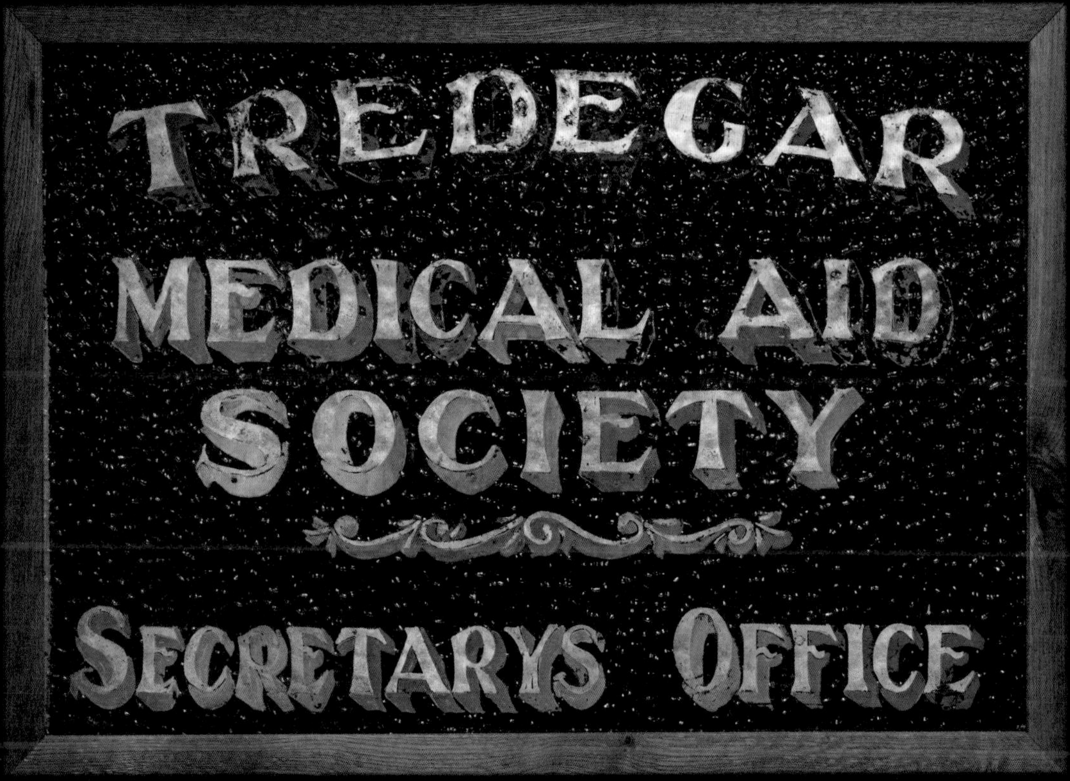
TREDEGAR
MEDICAL AID
SOCIETY
SECRETARYS OFFICE

87 Reading cards from Esgairdawe School
1927

Until 1870 Welsh children depended on a patchwork of Anglican and nonconformist schools for an elementary education – if they received one at all. The 1870 Education Act introduced non-sectarian elementary schools, publicly funded and governed by school boards. A school buildings programme began, and, though education was not compulsory until 1880, most children now attended school.

In 1877 a new school was opened in the remote Carmarthenshire hamlet of Esgairdawe. By June seventy children had enrolled. They often walked many miles to the new single-room school near the chapel. Attendance was not free: children paid 1d, 2d or 3d a week according to their age. An early pupil, D. Derwenydd Morgan, later recalled the first teacher, Robert Airey. 'He was a dyed-in-the-wool Englishman from the heart of that country. He knew no more Welsh than a goat knows the Greek alphabet. We illiterate children from the country couldn't understand a word he said. I'm not blaming the man. It was the board's intention to teach the children English, and of course to kill or drive out the Welsh language, if they could.'

In April 1878 an inspector reported that 'this new school has been brought into satisfactory order and discipline, and appears to be very fairly instructed'. But Mr Airey had problems. 'Some evenings, when he had money in his wallet', recalled Morgan, 'he would go to the pub [Tafarn Jem] and would be reeling drunk in no time. The next day the atmosphere in school wasn't good. His wallet was empty, his head hurt, and parts of his body ached as a result of Mrs Airey's "pugilistic power" '. The school faced other difficulties, including absenteeism as a result of illness, harsh weather and the competing needs of farming.

'Today the teacher informed the scholars,' according to the school logbook in 1887, 'that no more Welsh is to be spoken in school hours within the school premises.' The anti-Welsh tide only began to turn when O.M. Edwards, who had pioneered Welsh-language publications for children, became chief inspector of schools for Wales in 1907. Though most teaching was still in English, schools were expected to give more attention to reading and writing Welsh. In Esgairdawe the teacher from 1933 to 1942, Miss M.P. Reeves, insisted on Welsh skills, and the illustrated reading cards may date from her tenure. They were designed in 1927 by Ellen Evans, a pioneer of Welsh-medium education and principal of Barry Training College. She was one of the authors of an influential government report, *Welsh in Education and Life* (1927), and published children's stories in Welsh, paving the way for the popular *Llyfr Mawr y Plant*, which first appeared in 1931. In 1949 the inspector reported that Welsh was now the medium of instruction in Ysgol Esgairdawe.

The first (private) Welsh-medium school was opened in Aberystwyth in 1939 by Ifan ab Owen Edwards [90]. It was not until 1947 that the first state-funded Welsh-medium primary school, Ysgol Gymraeg Dewi Sant in Llanelli, was established.

Llyfr mawr y plant (National Library of Wales)

88 Brynmawr furniture
1930s

The economic depression that soon followed the end of the First World War bore down heavily on Wales. Demand slackened for the products of its two main industries, coal and iron, and agriculture languished.

As the surrounding collieries and ironworks closed down from 1925, Brynmawr, high on the northern fringe of the south Wales coalfield, suffered increasing levels of deprivation. Between 1932 and 1939 the town's unemployment rate was higher than anywhere else in Wales, with 90% of its insured men out of work.

Governments showed little or no interest in helping places like Brynmawr, and it was left to the people themselves and to outside groups to alleviate poverty and revive the economy. From 1926 groups of members of the Society of Friends (Quakers) came from England to Trealaw, Brynmawr and other coalfield towns to bring relief. They were not always welcomed. They tended to be seen as middle-class, alien and unsympathetic to the social, political and religious networks that sustained the community.

But in Brynmawr the Quakers persevered, under their able leader Peter Scott. They realised that their initial charitable relief work, providing food and clothes and building a new swimming pool, was not enough. What was needed was an 'attack on unemployment' itself. So began the 'Brynmawr Experiment'. In 1928 Scott and others began an economic and social survey, led by Hilda Jennings and published in 1934 as *Brynmawr: A Study of a Distressed Area*. It was compiled not by outside researchers, but co-operatively by some 150 Brynmawr residents.

In 1929 Scott and his colleagues re-opened a boot-making factory that had closed in 1926. In the same year they were joined by a young cabinet maker from London, Paul Matt, who started a new furniture factory, employing twelve workers as well as apprentices. Designs were simple in style, in keeping with Quaker values and contemporary modernist taste. The factory's manifesto stated: 'We exist to provide creative employment at not less than trade union rates of wages for men and boys who would otherwise be doomed to idleness and frustration. We strive to produce beautiful furniture of high quality and good design'.

Furniture was sold to Quakers, other supportive institutions and middle-class customers across Britain. As well as the Merthyr desk and Harlech chair (pictured) they could buy bookcases, sideboards, tables, chests of drawers and bureaus. Sales doubled every year for five years. In 1938 a chair was made for the Cardiff National Eisteddfod, strikingly plain in comparison with its elaborate predecessors.

In 1939 unemployment in Brynmawr still stood at 70%. For all its other achievements the experiment's effect on jobs was marginal. The Second World War put an end to the Brynmawr factory, but it also ended mass unemployment in the town. After 1945 the steel and textile industries offered many new jobs in the area. In Brynmawr a Labour peer and businessman, James Forrester, a volunteer with the Brynmawr Quakers from 1931, built a large rubber factory, assisted by a government grant. Its pioneering concrete building, designed by the Architects Co-operative Partnership and Ove Arup, included welfare and other facilities that unusually avoided social distinctions between managers and workers. Never a complete success, the factory was closed in 1982 and demolished in 2001.

89 Felinfoel beer can
1935

Thirst and heavy industry went together. Miners, tinplate workers and labourers in Llanelli had no lack of places to drink once their work was done. In 1896 there were said to be 45 public houses within 225 yards of the parish church. At first inns supplied their own beer, but soon commercial breweries sprang up. Buckley's Brewery had its origins in the eighteenth century, and just outside the town Felinfoel Brewery was established in 1878.

The founder of Felinfoel Brewery was David John. He worked as a coalminer and tinplate worker before leasing an old coaching inn in the village, the King's Head. From 1872 he brewed his own beer there, at first for his customers, then for other pubs. This venture was so successful that in 1878 he built a substantial new building, opposite the inn and astride the river Lliedi. The new plant produced beer, as well as 'Trebuan Spring' mineral water and ginger beer.

The Felinfoel Brewery survived many challenges, especially from the temperance movement, which was strong in Llanelli. From 1838 David Rees, the powerful minister of Capel Als, published and edited in the town *Y Dirwestwr Deheuol* (*The Southern Teetotaller*), a magazine arguing the case against drinking alcohol, seen as both a social and a moral evil. Later in the century teetotalism became part of mainstream nonconformist and Liberal doctrine. Campaigners achieved some success in 1881 with the Sunday Closing (Wales) Act, the first statute since the sixteenth century to apply to Wales alone. In August 1882 more than 4,000 people held a Great Temperance Demonstration in Llanelli, including a procession a mile long, to celebrate the passing of the Act and the closure of pubs on the Sabbath.

But workers continued to drink. The Felinfoel Brewery flourished. It acquired interests in two local firms, the Dafen Iron and Tinplate Works and the St David's Tinplate Works at Bynea. By now Llanelli had acquired the nickname 'Tinopolis', as the leading centre in Britain for manufacturing tinplate [48]. The link between brewing and tinplate was crucial in the Felinfoel Brewery's commercial development of the first canned beer to be made in Europe. In January 1935 two United States companies found a way of making a can that could withstand high pressure and avoid contaminating the beer's flavour. Felinfoel, working with tinplate from the St David's works and the Metal Box Company, soon followed. Its first cans appeared on 3 December 1935. A local newspaper headline announced, 'Canned beer arrives: epoch-making process at Felinfoel Brewery. New hope for tinplate industry'.

The first, half-pint cans were known as 'Brasso cans' because of their resemblance to Brasso metal polish tins. They had a conical upper section and a 'crown cork' bottle top. The cream coloured label listed the can's advantages: the beer was sealed, flavour preserved and harmful light excluded; cans were light to carry, they took up little space, and there were no deposits or returns. Before long, red replaced cream on the label, and the Felinfoel dragon appeared.

At first, sales of Felinfoel cans were modest. During the Second World War production increased, as cardboard boxes, each containing a dozen cans, were sent, post-free, to British troops abroad, especially in the Middle and Far East. Today canned beer is still brewed in Felinfoel, in the original building, by the same family firm.

90 Evacuee children at Newtown
1939

Between 1925 and 1939 almost 400,000 people left
Wales to escape unemployment and poverty. When the
Second World War began the population rose sharply,
by over 200,000 between 1939 and 1941, as new groups
arrived, including soldiers, government departments,
Land Girls, and part of the BBC. The largest group
consisted of child evacuees sent from cities and towns
in danger of being bombed by German aircraft. By 1945
about 110,000 children had been sent to Wales as part of
the UK-wide programme.

Detailed plans for evacuation were prepared in
1938. Even before war was declared on 3 September
1939 trains were bringing children from Liverpool and
elsewhere to Wales, most of which had been designated
as a reception area. One group was recorded arriving
at Newtown station by the news photographer Geoff
Charles on 1 or 2 September. Eric Jackson recalled,
'Along with dozens of other evacuees from Ionic
Street School at Rock Ferry [Birkenhead] we arrived
in Newtown. We each had a name and address label
secured to our outer garments, the obligatory gas masks
hanging from our necks and of course a small suitcase
with all our worldly goods – our few clothes.'

Evacuees lived with local families and attended
local schools. The social and psychological effects on
the children, many from urban slums, could be serious.
Being parted from their families was bad enough. Some
children were confused to find themselves in Welsh-
speaking villages. Others found it hard to get used to the
slow pace and nonconformist ways of their new homes.
Beryl Mathias, transported from Kent to west Wales,
recalled, 'Our religious knowledge lessons taught us that
hell was down below... but I knew it wasn't – it was in

that vicarage and those two stone-faced women were
the devil's disciples.' Others were warmly welcomed
and took quickly to their new surroundings. Barbara
Warlow Davies moved from blitzed Liverpool to a farm
at Talgarreg in Ceredigion, to live with 'Anti Rachel, who
cared for me better than any mother and taught me
skills I still remember'. Barbara was quickly assimilated:
'soon my command of Welsh had improved so much
that I was speaking to them like a local'.

The Welsh families receiving children were
sometimes shocked by their poor physical condition
and wild behaviour. Head lice were common. *The
Lancet* commented on frequent bed-wetting: 'Every
morning every window is filled with bedding, hung out
to dry in the sunshine. The scene is cheerful, but the
householders are depressed'. Some worried about what
effect the incomers would have on the Welsh language.
In autumn 1939 W.J. Gruffydd wrote of a village in
Arfon: 'On Saturday morning the first thing I saw was
the small children trying to gabble in English' with newly
arrived evacuees. It was the fear of large numbers of
Liverpool children descending on Aberystwyth that
persuaded Ifan ab Owen Edwards to begin a Welsh-
medium school in the town in September 1939 **[87]**. The
numbers of evacuees staying in Wales, though, proved
to be fewer than at first expected.

Geoff Charles was a gifted and prolific photo-
journalist. He worked for newspapers in north and mid
Wales from the mid-1930s to the 1970s, documenting
everyday life in detail. His photographs recorded not
only the arrival of the evacuees, but their subsequent
progress, in school, on country walks, playing football, in
Christmas parties, and listening to a hurdy-gurdy man.

91 Corgi toy car
1956

Philipp Ullmann owned a Nuremberg toy factory. Like other German Jews he feared the worst when Adolf Hitler came to power in January 1933 and fled to Britain. In Northampton, with a relative and fellow-refugee Arthur Katz, he founded the Mettoy Company Ltd and began producing metal toys from lithographed tin sheets. The business flourished.

When war began with Germany in September 1939 the government asked Mettoy to use their expertise to help the war effort. Toy production ceased in 1941, and the factory began making jerrycan components, shell fuses, Sten and Bren gun magazines, and landmines. When in 1944 the Ministry of Supply built a new factory at Fforestfach in Swansea, Mettoy were invited to occupy it and extend their weapons production.

When war ended in 1945 Mettoy returned to making toys. The company opened a large new factory at Fforestfach in 1949. By now it had developed high-capacity injection-moulding machinery and could produce toys in large numbers.

The Corgi range of toy vehicles, launched in 1956, cemented Mettoy's success. The name Corgi referred both to the native Welsh dogs and to the royal family's ownership of them. The first car produced was a Ford Consul saloon, sold in its distinctive Corgi box. It was followed by dozens of other models, not only cars but buses, tractors and petrol tankers. The 'Corgi Technocrat' engineers were noted for the precision of their detailing and their innovation. Cars soon had plastic windows – hence the slogan 'The One with Windows' – and other advanced features, like opening bonnets and boots, rubber tyres, friction motion and suspension. 'Masterpieces of Lilliputian engineering' was one description of them. Special editions were popular, like James Bond's Aston Martin DB5 of 1965. Corgis were a huge success among Britain's baby boom children. At the end of the 1950s they were being exported to over 100 countries. In 1968 3,500 people were employed at Fforestfach.

Women made up much of the workforce. Most worked on the assembly lines; few were managers or technical staff. Remembering their days at Fforestfach, some women valued the friendships and solidarity in the factory. For Cynthia Rix, 'Mettoys was the love of my life. There was fairness there, there was togetherness there'. Others hated the monotony and discipline. Annest Wiliam feared for her colleagues when the time-and-motion man arrived: 'They all had to sort of smarten up, it was like it was a test, an exam on them personally'.

Falling sales, competition from cheaper manufacturers abroad and the failure of its Dragon 32 computer led to Mettoy closing its Fforestfach plant in 1983. The other large toy factory in Wales, Triang in Merthyr Tydfil, had already closed.

Over the years 'real' cars have also been made in Wales – both car parts and entire cars. Between 1959 and 1973 the Gilbern company, a partnership of a Welsh butcher and German engineer, produced GT cars from its base at Llantwit Fardre. Aston Martin plan to begin production of luxury cars at St Athan in 2019.

Women Mettoy workers (Swansea Museum)

CORGI TOYS

CORGI TOYS

CORGI TOYS

CORGI TOYS

200

FORD CONSUL
SALOON

TRANS·O·LITE
HEADLAMPS

SPRING
SUSPENSION.
STEERING WHEEL
SEATS.

205

RILEY PATHFINDER
SALOON

92 Penrhiwceiber Lodge banner
1960s

After the 'locust years' of the 1930s, with their pit closures, means tests and poverty, Welsh coalminers could be more hopeful after 1945. The Labour government nationalised the coal industry in 1947, putting an end to the dominance of the large coal companies. Investment in the industry increased, and wages and conditions improved. The Miners' Eisteddfod and Miner's Gala, both post-war innovations, testified to the continuing vitality of the miners' collective culture.

A visible symbol of that culture was the banner. Banners were carried at political and social events, and in marches and demonstrations. In February 1935 miners and others had carried banners during a mass protest against the government's cuts in unemployment pay. Fifty thousand people marched down the Cynon Valley to Mountain Ash, in a procession two and a half miles long. 'The world's brow was hot', wrote the novelist Gwyn Thomas, who was there, 'and we were out to fan it with banners'. In the 1950s lodge banners began to be made. The miners of several Cynon Valley lodges, including Penrhiwceiber, designed one featuring the slogan 'Knowledge is power' and the image of a miner holding a book and a globe. In the 1960s Penrhiwceiber Lodge commissioned a new, more striking banner with the same device.

Books were a symbol of learning. But they also referred to the libraries, over a hundred by 1934, built by the miners to advance their education and culture. They have been described as 'one of the greatest networks of cultural institutions created by working people anywhere in the world'. The libraries had pride of place in new miners' institutes. By the 1920s most coalfield towns and many villages could boast an institute, which acted as a centre for the whole local community. The workmen's institute and public hall in Penrhiwceiber was built in 1888 with financial help from the owners of Penrikyber Colliery. It later became the property of the miners. As well as a cinema, meeting and billiard rooms it included a library and reading room, which were so well developed by 1903 that the village turned down an offer of £700 by Andrew Carnegie to build a public library.

The libraries included general books, but also more radical political and economic reading. Aneurin Bevan [86] recalled, 'I was especially fortunate in the quality of the library [in the Tredegar Institute] which had been built up by the pennies of the miners ... they made available to us both the orthodox economists and philosophers, and the Marxist source books.' Some miners ventured beyond self-education, attending classes, local and residential, organised by the Plebs League, the Workers' Educational Association, Ruskin College, the Central Labour College and Coleg Harlech. Like Bevan they often went on to become union and political leaders.

The globe on the banner recalls the coalfield tradition of internationalism. South Wales miners supplied aid to Spain during the Spanish Civil War (1936-39) and 122 of them fought with the International Brigades in defence of the Republic.

Mountain Ash and Penrhiwceiber Lodges banner
(South Wales Miners' Library)

SOUTH WALES AREA N.U.M
PENRHIWCEIBER LODGE
"KNOWLEDGE IS POWER"

93 The Pontypool front row
c.1978

If football was the predominant organised sport in north Wales **[81]**, rugby ruled in the south. It was an upper-class game in England and, at first, in Wales – Llandovery and Lampeter colleges were pioneers in the 1850s. But the sport was quickly taken up by workers in the expanding industrial towns. Local clubs grew up from 1871. 1881 saw the foundation of the Welsh Rugby Union and the first Wales international game, against England, played in Blackheath.

The first golden age of Welsh rugby was between 1900 and 1911, when Wales won six Triple Crowns. In December 1905 Wales defeated New Zealand **[68]**, a victory seen as a symbol of a confident, successful Edwardian Wales. In the interwar years the fortunes of rugby reflected the country's economic and social decline. The population fell, crowds dwindled, and players 'went north' to play professional rugby league in Lancashire and Yorkshire.

After the Second World War rugby revived. From the mid-1960s the Welsh team regained some of its earlier brio. Public interest was buoyed by television coverage and the songs and jokes of Max Boyce. In 1967 John Hughes found a receptive market when he began to produce ceramic figures of rugby players from his workshop in Treforest near Pontypridd. He moulded and painted by hand each resin figure, which he called a 'Grogg'. In 1971 he bought a disused local pub as a studio and shop, and the business grew, especially as Welsh rugby entered its second golden age, between 1969 and 1980.

The success of the 1970s Welsh team – it won three Grand Slams and six Triple Crowns – was founded on a strong network of clubs led by talented coaches like Carwyn James of Llanelli. Gifted half-backs like Barry John, Gareth Edwards and Phil Bennett could rely on a powerful pack of forwards. The pack was fronted by three Pontypool players, Graham Price, Bobby Windsor and Charlie Faulkner (Windsor and Faulkner were both steelworkers). At Pontypool Ray Prosser, the club coach between 1969 and 1987, insisted on complete player fitness and moulded a powerful team that won the unofficial club championship five times. The Pontypool front row combined strength with discipline to defeat most opposition packs. Between 1975 and 1979 the three played together 19 times for Wales, on the winning side on all but four occasions, and they played for the British Lions.

The distinctive, battle-hardened features of the trio made them ideal Groggs (John Hughes claimed that he found making 'handsome' characters harder). Gareth Edwards was the best-selling figure, and rugby players still form the largest group of Groggs, now produced by John Hughes's son, Richard. When Gareth Bale became the first Welsh footballer to sell more Grogg copies than any contemporary Welsh rugby player, a change was taking place in the relative standing and popularity of the two games.

Rugby union became a professional game in 1995, and financial pressures led to the restructuring of the Welsh clubs. Finally only four clubs, all based in the coastal belt, remained at the top level. Attendances at their matches have declined. Pontypool now play in the third tier of club rugby. Meanwhile football gained more followers, especially after 2011, when the Premier League included a Welsh club, and 2016, when the Wales team performed well in the European Championship.

GRAHAM PRICE BOBBY WINDSOR CHARLIE FAULKNER

94. Laura Ashley dress
1970s

For centuries wool was a staple of the Montgomeryshire economy. The main product of the mills of Newtown, Llanidloes and other towns was cheap flannel, a soft cloth woven from carded wool. Larger mills emerged, exporting products to England and overseas (some crossed the Atlantic as clothes for slaves). By 1831 Newtown's population had risen to 4,550, and a new Flannel Exchange was being built. The 1830s brought a depression, which caused distress and social conflict [61], but the industry recovered. Flannel was at the heart of the first large-scale mail-order business in Britain, built by Pryce Pryce-Jones in Newtown from the 1870s. But in the end Montgomeryshire could not compete with the mills of northern England, and by 1900 little remained of the industry.

When Laura Ashley brought her small textile business to Machynlleth in 1961 she may have been in search of cheaper labour rather than a revival of the county's textile industry, but her move did lead to a small renaissance. Laura Mountney was born in Dowlais in 1925. Though she was brought up in Surrey she returned to Dowlais for regular holidays, and recalled watching her great aunts making quilts on a quilting frame [72]. Inspired by them and by traditional patterns she found in her research, she began printing headscarves and tea towels on her kitchen table in Pimlico, helped by her husband Bernard, who operated a silkscreen printer. These began to find a market, and Laura persuaded Bernard to move to Wales.

The house in Machynlleth soon proved too small, and in 1966 the Ashleys bought new accommodation in Carno, a small village 18 miles to the east. Here they soon took over the disused railway station building and turned it into a factory making cotton tea towels, smocks, dresses, blouses and other items. They employed over a hundred people. According to one worker, 'they breathed life back into the village', which had long suffered from a lack of jobs. The business flourished, helped by the complementary skills of Laura's creativity and Bernard's business acumen. A Laura Ashley shop was opened in London in 1968. By now taste in women's fashion was moving away from the short lengths, bold colours and artificial fabrics of the early 1960s towards a looser and more rural look captured by Laura's phrase 'the security of nostalgia'. She was quick to exploit the new mood, hunting down Victorian designs, like those she found in Owen Jones's pattern book *The Grammar of Ornament* (1856), and reviving them in modernised form. The firm grew rapidly. The Ashleys opened more factories, including ones in Newtown and Machynlleth, and by 1985 they owned 220 shops across the world.

In its early years the Carno factory was closely supervised by the Ashleys. Pay was modest and unions banned, but conditions, at Laura's insistence, were 'maternalistic'. Hours were flexible to allow for child care, the working week ended at lunchtime on Friday, home-working was possible, and buses were provided to transport the employees.

After Laura Ashley died in an accident in 1985 the company began to decline, despite diversifying into furniture and interior decoration. Tastes had moved on again, and the Laura Ashley brand no longer held the same magnetism. In 1998 the company was taken over by a Malaysian firm and its commitment to Wales waned. The Carno factory closed in 2005.

95 SuperTed
c.1980

SuperTed was no ordinary bear. He once lay forgotten and afraid of the dark, but Mother Nature gave him supernatural powers. On whispering the secret magic word he was transformed into a superhero, with red cape and rocket boots, ready to join his friend Spotty and do battle with his wicked enemies, Texas Pete, Bulk and Skeleton.

SuperTed is unusual for another reason. He appeared first in a series of bedtime stories created in 1978 by Barry-born Mike Young to help his young stepson go to sleep. After a series of successful books, Young joined others in setting up a company, Siriol Productions, to make animated films of SuperTed's adventures. Siriol agreed to produce them in Welsh for the newly-established Sianel Pedwar Cymru (S4C). A *SuperTed* cartoon was the first programme to be broadcast when S4C began transmitting on 1 November 1982 – in part a symbol of the new channel's determination to appeal to young audiences.

Many thought that a Welsh-language television channel would never see the light of day. BBC Radio Cymru, the first radio station to broadcast entirely in Welsh, had begun in 1977. But the campaign to persuade the government to provide Wales with a television equivalent, seen as essential for the survival of Welsh as a living language, was long and difficult. After the 1979 general election the Conservative government broke a manifesto promise to set up such a channel. The response in Wales was angry. Protestors began a campaign of civil disobedience, which included a refusal to pay the television licence fee and attacks on television transmitters. Gwynfor Evans, president of Plaid Cymru, threatened to starve himself to death unless the government relented. Finally, fearful of the likely public reaction if Evans were to die, the government capitulated and agreed to set up and fund the new channel.

Before he appeared first on television SuperTed had been recreated as a soft toy. He was originally coloured blue, with red cape, belt and boots. But Warner Brothers warned Mike Young that he would be infringing copyright, since another famous superhero wore the same colours. The case went to court, and for a short time SuperTed turned black. When Young won the case, his bear changed colour again, to red. It was the red SuperTed who achieved fame, in Welsh, in English and in many other languages, as he circled the earth during the next few years.

For S4C, working with a minority language but keen to make a mark internationally, animation was an attractive medium. With a changed soundtrack, an animated film could cross linguistic and national barriers with ease. The channel commissioned new series, including *Wil Cwac Cwac*, *Fireman Sam* and *Gogs*. Later, longer, more ambitious works were made, often as co-productions with other countries, such as *Shakespeare: The Animated Tales*, the product of a Wales-Russia partnership, and *The Canterbury Tales*. Siriol produced an animated version of Dylan Thomas's *Under Milk Wood*, and Cartwn Cymru *Y Mabinogi*. These and other films gained international reputations. As S4C's funds shrank Welsh animation declined, but animators and their trainers are still at work in Cardiff.

Cardiff is where animation began in Wales, in 1925. Sid Griffiths, a cinema projectionist, created the mischievous but knowing cartoon dog Jerry the Tyke. His short silent films are inventive and playful.

96 Badges from the miners' strike
1984-85

The defeat of the miners in the 1984-85 coal dispute led to the virtual end of an industry that had dominated parts of Wales for a century, and put an end to the powerful influence of organised industrial labour.

Margaret Thatcher's government was determined to abolish coal subsidies, to subject the industry to global market forces, and to destroy the power of the National Union of Mineworkers (NUM). On becoming prime minister in 1979, Thatcher said privately, 'The last Conservative government was destroyed by the miners' strike. We'll have another one and we'll win.' The government appointed Ian MacGregor, an industrial director with a reputation for ruthlessness, to chair British Coal. It also stockpiled supplies of coal, changed employment and social security law to disadvantage strikers, and prepared police forces to counter expected resistance. The NUM leader Arthur Scargill also welcomed conflict, as a chance to defeat a hostile government.

When the government announced the closure of 20 pits Scargill called for a strike in March 1984. There was no majority in favour – the 20,000 miners in Wales were mainly against – but the strike went ahead. After some initial reluctance the south Wales miners proved the most solid in their support. The conflict was prolonged, bitter and sometimes violent. It ended in a comprehensive defeat for the miners, as the government used all its economic, legal and coercive power to prevail.

The Welsh miners were defending not only their jobs but also their culture and communities. In turn those communities supported the strikers. Women organised locally, to collect and distribute food and to gather further support. In Newbridge Dot Phillips led a women's support group. Interviewed in 2014, she recalled with pride setting up soup kitchens for the miners in the two local Celynen collieries, raising money and speaking in meetings across the country. 'That sense of togetherness,' she wrote earlier, 'is an experience I cannot forget'.

Support groups sprang up far outside the coalfields. In Wales help came from quarry workers, farmers, churches and ethnic minority groups. Groups were set up in Oxford, Liverpool, Bristol and other English cities, and help came from overseas. The 2014 film *Pride* recalls the help given to miners in the Dulais valley by a London gay and lesbian group led by Mark Ashton and Mike Jackson. One of the group's fundraising gigs was called 'Pits and Perverts', a phrase allegedly borrowed from *The Sun* newspaper. From the solidarity groups begun during the strike arose a new generation of grassroots activists, especially women, who contributed to many later social movements.

A ubiquitous symbol of identity and solidarity during the strike was the badge. Hundreds of different badges were produced during the year, many of them by individual union lodges. The enamel Penrhiwceiber badge, sold to raise funds, incorporated the 'knowledge is power' motto familiar from the lodge's banners [92]. Others were made by support groups, like the badge produced by Portsmouth Polytechnic Students Union in support of Celynen South miners.

The strikers, defeated, returned to work in March 1985. Within months British Coal closed many Welsh mines, including Penrhiwceiber and both Celynen pits. Tower Colliery near Hirwaun was closed in 1994, but its workers, led by Tyrone O'Sullivan, bought the pit from British Coal and production resumed. The last deep mine to operate in Wales, Tower finally closed in 2008.

RHYMNEY VALLEY MINERS SUPPORT GROUP
1984 1985
CYDLYNIAD

TRELEWIS DRIFT · SOUTH WALES AREA
NUM
1984 STRIKE

DIG
DEEP FOR
THE
MINERS!

G.C.G. WOMEN
SUPPORT
THE MINERS

SUPPORT THE MINERS
NUM
STOP PIT CLOSURES

UPPER RHONDDA CENTRE
MINERS STRIKE 1984-85

GARW VALLEY
STRIKE 1984-85

LADY WINDSOR
MINERS STRIKE
1984 1985
SOUTH NUM WALES

nga
SOLIDARITY WITH THE
MINERS
1984-85
STRIKE

MARDY
NUM
1984
LAST PIT IN THE RHONDDA

OAKDALE NAVIGATION LODGE
52 WEEKS SOLIDARITY
NUM
1984/85 STRIKE

PENRIKYBER
A PIT WORTH SAVING

97 Catatonia's first record
1993

From 1899, when Madge Breeze recorded 'Hen Wlad Fy Nhadau' [68], singers and instrumentalists from Wales have made music recordings in ever increasing numbers. Between 1910 and 1914 Ruth Herbert Lewis used an Edison Bell 'Gem' phonograph to make over 150 pioneering recordings on wax cylinders of Welsh traditional folk musicians in the field in north Wales, with transcription help from the talented young composer Morfydd Llwyn Owen.

Popular music too has a long recording history. For many years it flowed in two parallel streams. English-language singers and groups could often command an audience beyond Wales. The music of Welsh-language performers tended to travel less widely, but a lively network grew up to meet their needs within Wales – recording companies like Sain, Fflach and Ankst, venues and festivals like Clwb Ifor Bach and Y Sesiwn Fawr, and magazines such as *Sothach* and *Y Selar*. Radical bands like Datblygu and Anrhefn won cult followings, occasionally outside Wales.

This pattern began to change in the 1990s, as Welsh-medium musicians set their sights on wider audiences more willing to explore different kinds of music. One of the first bands to cross the divide was Catatonia, led by Cerys Matthews and Mark Roberts, who had played guitar with the Welsh-language band Y Cyrff. The band's first gig was in Clwb Ifor Bach. In May 1993 Crai, an offshoot of Sain, released their first CD record, an EP with five songs. Rhys Mwyn of Crai overcame his initial doubts about featuring 'For Tinkerbell', an English-language song about the loss of innocence, as the lead song on the record. There were two other English songs, 'New Mercurial Heights' and 'Sweet Catatonia', and two

in Welsh, 'Gyda Gwên' and 'Dimbran'. All the songs were written by Roberts and Matthews. Cerys Matthews's voice, quietly winsome one moment, gravelly and raucous the next, combined with the band's powerful guitar sound and oblique lyrics to catch the attention of DJs and magazine writers. So did Rolant Dafis' cover photo, featuring an innocent-looking cherub found in a Hypervalue shop.

Catatonia's second album, *International Velvet*, released in 1997, reached a large audience and sold over 900,000 copies in 22 months. Five of its songs were successfully issued as singles, including 'Mulder and Scully' and 'Road Rage'.

Other 'bilingual' Welsh bands became household names around the same time. Super Furry Animals, with Gruff Rhys as lead singer and guitarist, became known for irreverent psychedelia, while Gorki's Zygotic Mynci, from Carmarthen, mixed Welsh and English-language songs that gained a cult appeal. For all these bands the road to wider recognition had already been paved by the Manic Street Preachers, a band from Blackwood. Their sound was harsher, and they sang of personal anguish as well as political resistance. The band survived the disappearance in 1995 of its lead singer Richey Edwards and continued to produce albums into the 2010s.

Welsh musicians still record abundantly, both within their own traditions and in collaboration with musicians from different cultures. The harpist Catrin Finch has released records with the Senegalese kora player Seckou Keita, and Gwyneth Glyn recorded with the Indian singer Tauseef Akhtar.

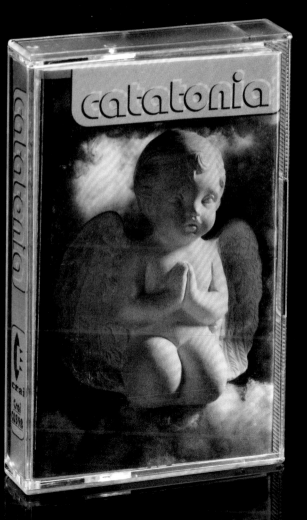

98 'Yes' campaign poster
1997

The Cymru Fydd movement within the Liberal Party, the first modern attempt to bring self-government to Wales, collapsed in 1896. Over the next hundred years efforts to revive the idea came to nothing. Plaid Cymru, founded in 1925 as the Welsh Nationalist Party, aimed for political independence, and the Liberal Party came in time to favour devolving power. But the Conservatives were consistently unionist in outlook, and the Labour Party, despite campaigns by individuals like E.T. John, Jim Griffiths and S.O. Davies, was largely hostile to devolution, at least until the mid-1970s. In the referendum held in March 1979 almost 80% of those voting rejected the setting up of a Welsh Assembly.

By 1997 much had changed. Conservative governments had been in power in Westminster continuously for eighteen years, but most Welsh voters had never voted for them. Their lack of a democratic mandate in Wales was clear, and their policies were widely resented [96]. The Welsh Labour Party, the dominant electoral force in Wales, became convinced that devolution of power was necessary. Tony Blair's Labour government, which came to power in May 1997, fulfilled its promise to hold a second referendum on whether to set up a Welsh Assembly. The vote was called for 18 September 1997.

A powerful cross-party consensus, excluding the Conservatives, was built in favour of devolution. Its architect was Ron Davies, Secretary of State for Wales in the new government. The 'Yes for Wales' campaign, formed before the general election in February 1997, attracted many supporters outside politics, including rugby players, writers, musicians (including Catatonia [97] and the Stereophonics), and visual artists. One of the most prominent artists was the Ceredigion painter Mary Lloyd Jones. She painted two large banners in her characteristic style, which uses irregular and mobile patches of bright colours and often fragments of text – in this case the simple message 'Yes / Ie'. The banners appeared at rallies and at the National Eisteddfod in Bala. She also produced posters with the lettering 'Say Yes for Wales / *Dywedwch Ie dros Gymru*' (the copy in Storiel was donated by Ron Davies).

The 'No' campaigns, led by Conservatives and dissenting Labour Party members, were weaker and poorly organised, but popular opinion was evenly divided. In Scotland, where a similar devolution referendum was held on 11 September, a cross-party Constitutional Convention had mobilised public opinion for devolution since 1989, and the outcome there was never in doubt. In Wales only half of the electorate voted. The outcome was unclear until the results from the last county, Carmarthenshire, were announced. 'Yes' won by just 6,721 votes.

After the referendum the Government of Wales Act set up the National Assembly. Its sixty members, elected in part by proportional representation, began work in May 1999. The use of the preposition 'for', rather than 'of' in 'National Assembly for Wales' revealed much about its top-down origin and lack of popular ownership. Years passed before most people felt an affinity to the new body. At first it had no lawmaking powers or ability to raise taxes – powers devolved gradually from Westminster over the years. But slowly it found a distinctive course [100]. As Ron Davies wrote in 1999: 'Devolution is a process. It is not an event and neither is it a journey with a fixed end-point'.

SAY YES FOR WALES

canfos. rhodd Fedwen Tentage

99 Raspberry Pi *Mark 1, model B, revision 2*
2011

The networked computer was critical to early twenty-first century Wales. A machine able to process large amounts of information, and connected to millions of other computers and data stores, transformed economic and social life. Satellite navigation, search engines, online shopping, digital libraries, social networking – all were unknown only a few years before.

As traditional jobs decayed, the new information economy increased demand for computer and information-handling skills. But in the late 1990s the teaching of computing had almost vanished from British schools, replaced by a narrow concentration on using basic tools like word-processors and spreadsheets. At the end of the 2000s a reaction set in. Industry and teachers started to demand that programming skills and computing principles be restored to the curriculum. In Wales, Computing at School and Technocamps promoted computer studies in schools and added to the pressure.

In 2012 Eben Upton, a Cambridge University computer scientist born in Pontypool, unveiled a cheap and simple computer aimed at helping children learn how to code. He called it the Raspberry Pi. Its 'bare bones' circuit board was no larger than a credit card but it was powerful and it could be connected to a keyboard, mouse, display, camera and the internet. Above all, it was fully programmable. Coders could use it to control drones, devise video games, build weather stations, make robots and create for themselves a thousand other devices. Upton was surprised by the huge demand for Raspberry Pis, from computer experts as well as learners, and from developing as well as developed countries. At first they were made in China, but in 2012 engineers at Sony in Pencoed near Bridgend persuaded the Raspberry Pi

Foundation that Sony could produce them better in Wales – a reversal of the normal trend of exporting manufacturing jobs to low-wage countries.

Sony was first attracted to Bridgend in 1973, at a time when the UK government was beginning to persuade large overseas companies to invest in Wales (the Welsh Development Agency began work in 1976.) The factory concentrated on producing television sets and at its peak employed over 4,000 workers. Over time, though, demand declined and the Bridgend plant closed in 2005. But the Pencoed centre specialised in digital technologies and was already making equipment like specialist cameras when the Raspberry Pi contract began.

Since 2012 Sony has made over 15m Raspberry Pi computers, using advanced robots to make production processes faster and more accurate. Human workers carry out demanding work requiring higher engineering skills – in contrast to the pattern of the earlier television factory, which used more assembly line workers but lacked higher-skilled staff engaged in research and development.

'When we started Raspberry Pi', Eben Upton says, 'we never imagined we'd sell over ten million units, and we certainly never imagined that we'd be able to build those units in South Wales. Spending my summers in Pontypool as a child, I was surrounded by evidence of south Wales's manufacturing heritage; it's been a highlight of my adult life to be able to contribute in a small way to sustaining that heritage.' His Raspberry Pi Foundation supports local workshops, 'Raspberry Jams', and a large programme to encourage children to take an interest in computer programming, setting up 'coding clubs' in schools throughout Wales, Britain and overseas. Small firms also sprang up selling add-ons to the Raspberry Pi.

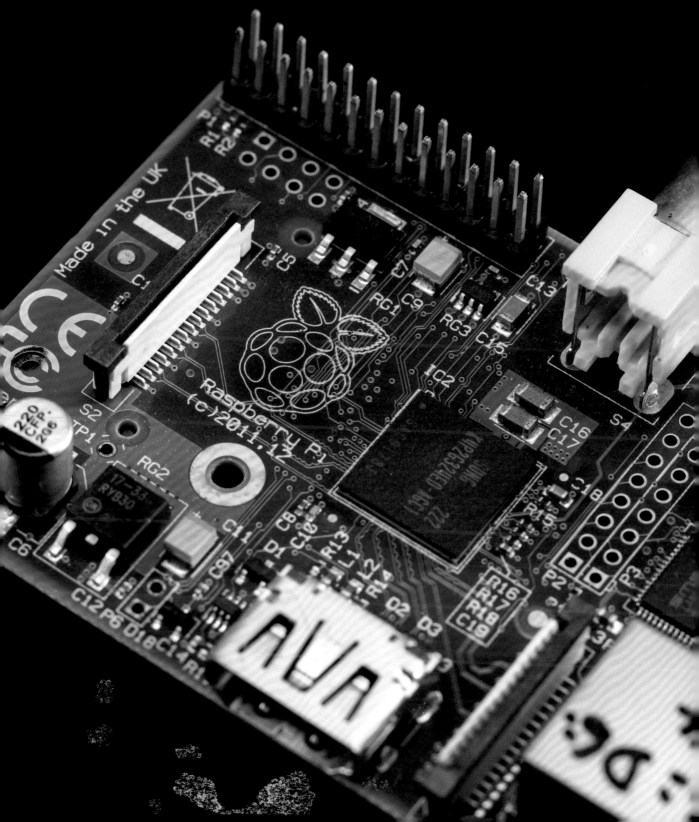

100 Wales Coast Path waymarker
2012

In June 2005 Rhodri Morgan, the First Minister of Wales, announced plans for an ambitious project, championed by Jane Davidson, one of his Cabinet ministers, to open a public footpath round the entire coastline of Wales. 'The economic benefits of access to the Welsh coast are self-evident', he said, 'and tourism is the major industry in many of our coastal resorts. But encouraging and enabling more people to enjoy physical recreation at the coast can also help in our efforts to become a fitter, healthier nation.' In May 2012 the 1,400km Wales Coast Path was opened. Wales became the country with the longest continuous path round its coastline.

Building the Path was a large undertaking for the Countryside Commission for Wales and its partners, including Welsh local authorities, national parks, the Welsh Government, and the Ramblers, who campaigned for it and built many of its stiles and gates. Where rights of way did not already exist, the planners negotiated access with landowners. They built 250 stiles, 1,282 gates, 159 bridges and 169 boardwalks. They put up directional signs, recognisable by their blue and yellow colours and white, dragon-tail conch.

Parts of the path were already in place, notably the Pembrokeshire Coast Path. This owed its existence to a single man, the naturalist Ronald M. Lockley. From 1927 to 1940 Lockley lived on Skokholm, off the Pembrokeshire coast, and set up there the UK's first bird observatory. He was a prolific author, writing influential accounts of the Manx shearwater and the rabbit, and in 1938, with Julian Huxley, he made one of the first British documentary nature films, *The Private Life of the Gannets*. After the Pembrokeshire Coast National Park was designated in 1952 he conceived the idea of a coastal path, surveyed the route himself, and wrote a report for the Countryside Commission. It took another seventeen years before the Path was opened, in 1970.

The Wales Coast Path planners were also helped by the fact that the National Trust already owned over 150 miles of coastline, accumulated gradually since the introduction of its 'Enterprise Neptune' programme in 1965.

A total of £15m was spent in creating the path, with a substantial grant from the European Union. Researchers soon found that its benefits far outweighed the cost. In 2014 about 43.4m visits were made to the path, 41% of them by people from outside Wales, and £401m was spent with local businesses. All told, 71km of new path had been opened up to people with mobility difficulties. Economists estimate that the health benefits of walking the path equated to £11.3m a year.

The Wales Coast Path is one of several pioneering measures made by Welsh governments since the formation of the National Assembly **[98]**. Others include a ban on smoking in public places, free bus passes for the over-60s, free prescriptions, waste recycling schemes and a 'deemed consent' system of organ donation. Policies on education and health diverged from those of England, as Welsh governments sought to keep public services free of private and commercial interests. But many areas of government, like police and the courts, energy policy, broadcasting and most taxation remain under the control of the UK government. And Welsh governments are relatively powerless to influence the performance of the Welsh economy, which is yet to bring the improvements in prosperity and well-being that many hoped for when the Assembly began.

Llwybr Arfordir
Coast Path

Aberarth 1
Llanon 4

Llwybr Arfordir Cymru
Wales Coast Path

MAP OF LOCATIONS

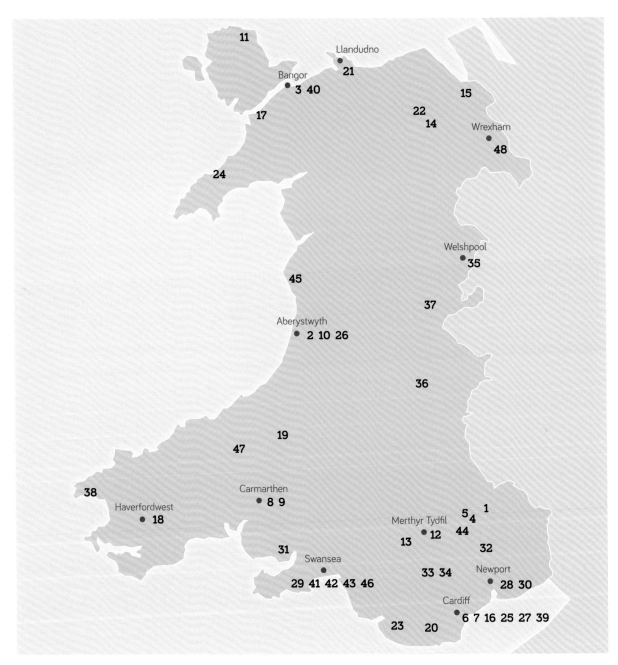

11

Llandudno
21

Bangor
3 40

17

15

22
14

Wrexham
48

24

Welshpool
35

45

37

Aberystwyth
2 10 26

36

19

47

38

Carmarthen
8 9

Haverfordwest
18

31

Swansea
29 41 42 43 46

Merthyr Tydfil
12

13

5 4
44

1

32

33 34

Newport
28 30

Cardiff
6 7 16 25 27 39

23

20

LIST OF LOCATIONS

12 Cyfarthfa Castle Museum
and Art Gallery
Brecon Road
Merthyr Tydfil
CF47 8RE
cyfarthfa.com
55 55 inset **61** inset **70 70** inset

13 Cynon Valley Museum
Depot Road
Aberdare
Rhondda Cynon Taf
CF44 8DL
cynonvalleymuseum.org
92

14 Denbighshire Archives
The Old Gaol
46 Clwyd Street
Ruthin
Denbighshire
LL15 1HP
archives.denbighshire.gov.uk
32

15 Flintshire Record Office
The Old Rectory
Rectory Lane
Hawarden
Flintshire
CH5 3NR
www.flintshire.gov.uk
73 inset

16 Glamorgan Archives
Clos Parc Morgannwg
Leckwith
Cardiff

CF11 8AW
glamarchives.gov.uk
34 40

17 Gwynedd Archives Service
Caernarfon Record Office
Gwynedd Council
Caernarfon
Gwynedd
LL55 1SH
gwynedd.llyw.cymru
76 inset

18 Haverfordwest Town Museum
Castle House
Castle Street
Haverfordwest
Pembrokeshire
SA61 2EF
haverfordwest-town-museum.
org.uk
24 24 inset **37**

19 Jen Jones Welsh Quilts and
Blankets
Pontbrendu
Llanybydder
Ceredigion
SA40 9UJ
jen-jones.com
72

20 Llancarfan, St Cadoc's Church
Llancarfan
Vale of Glamorgan
CF62 3AJ
stcadocs.org.uk
28

21 Llandudno Museum
17-19 Gloddaeth Street
Llandudno
Conwy
LL30 2DD
llandudnomuseum.co.uk
17 29

22 Llanrhaeadr-yng-Nghinmeirch,
St Dyfnog's Church
Bryn Llan
Llanrhaeadr-yng-Nghinmeirch
Denbighshire
LL16 4NN
stdyfnog.org.uk
27 inset

23 Llantwit Major, St Illtud's Church
College Street
Llantwit Major
Vale of Glamorgan
CF61 1SG
llanilltud.org.uk
18

24 Llŷn Maritime Museum
St Mary's Church
Stryd y Mynach
Nefyn
Gwynedd
LL53 6LB
llyn-maritime-museum.co.uk
63

25 National Assembly for Wales
Senedd
Cardiff Bay
Cardiff

CF99 1NA
assembly.wales
2 inset

26 **National Library of Wales**
Aberystwyth
Ceredigion
SY23 3BU
library.wales
20 22 inset **23 26 28** inset
35 36 38 44 inset **45 47 49** inset
52 53 inset **62 64 65 68 69 71 74**
77 78 79 inset **80** inset **84** inset
87 inset **90 97**

27 **National Museum Cardiff**
Cathays Park
Cardiff
CF10 3NP
museum.wales/cardiff
44 56 60

National Museum Wales
museum.wales
See Big Pit National Coal
Museum, National Museum
Cardiff, National Roman Legion
Museum, National Waterfront
Museum, St Fagans National
Museum of Welsh History

28 **National Roman Legion Museum**
High Street
Caerleon
Newport
NP18 1AE
museum.wales/roman
12

29 **National Waterfront Museum**
Oystermouth Road
Maritime Quarter
Swansea
SA1 3RD
museum.wales/swansea
67 80 83 99

30 **Newport Museum and Art Gallery**
John Frost Square
Newport
NP20 1PA
www.newport.gov.uk/heritage
11 61

31 **Parc Howard Museum**
and Art Gallery
Felinfoel Road
Llanelli
Carmarthenshire
SA15 3LJ
carmarthenshire.gov.wales
89

32 **Pontypool Museum**
Torfaen Museum Trust
Park Buildings
Pontypool
Torfaen
NP4 6JH
pontypoolmuseum.org.uk
48 93

33 **Pontypridd, Ynysangharad Park**
Ceridwen Terrace
Pontypridd
Rhondda Cynon Taf
CF37 4PD

rctcbc.gov.uk
68 inset

34 **Pontypridd Museum**
Bridge Street
Pontypridd
Rhondda Cynon Taf
CF37 4PE
pontypriddmuseum.cymru
54

35 **Powysland Museum**
The Canal Wharf
Severn Street
Welshpool
Powys
SY21 7AQ
powys.gov.uk/powyslandmuseum
51 94

36 **Radnorshire Museum**
Temple Street
Llandrindod Wells
Powys
LD1 5DL
powys.gov.uk
radnorshiremuseum
66 66 inset

37 **Robert Owen Museum**
The Cross
Broad Street
Newtown
Powys
SY16 2BB
robert-owen-museum.org.uk
85 inset

38 St Davids Cathedral
St Davids
Pembrokeshire
SA62 6RD
stdavidscathedral.org.uk
31

**39 St Fagans National Museum
of History**
St Fagans
Cardiff
CF5 6XB
**1 3 4 5 6 7 8 13 15 19 21 22 25 30
33** inset **46 46** inset **59 62** inset
75 82

40 Storiel
Ffordd Gwynedd
Bangor
Gwynedd
LL57 1DT
gwynedd.llyw.cymru
9 43 98

41 Swansea Museum
Victoria Road
Maritime Quarter
Swansea
SA1 1SN
swanseamuseum.co.uk
2 67 91 inset

**42 Swansea University,
Richard Burton Archives**
Singleton Park Library
Swansea University
Singleton Park
Swansea

SA2 8PP
swansea.ac.uk/library/archive-
and-research-collections
85

**43 Swansea University,
South Wales Miners' Library**
Hendrefoelan Campus
Gower Road
Swansea
SA2 7NB
swansea.ac.uk/iss/swml
92 inset

44 Tredegar Museum
Tredegar Library
The Circle
Tredegar
Blaenau Gwent
NP22 3PS
tredegarmuseum.co.uk
86

45 Tywyn, St Cadfan's Church
College Green
Tywyn
Gwynedd
LL36 9BS
stcadfantywyn.org.uk
16

**46 West Glamorgan Archives
Service**
Civic Centre
Oystermouth Road
Swansea
SA1 3SN
swansea.gov.uk/

westglamorganarchives
57

**47 West Wales Museum
of Childhood**
Pen-ffynnon
Llangeler
Carmarthenshire
SA44 5EY
toymuseumwales.co.uk
91 95

**48 Wrexham County Borough
Museum**
County Buildings
Regent Street
Wrexham
LL11 1RB
wrexham.gov.uk/english/heritage
81

ACKNOWLEDGEMENTS

Many institutions and many people have contributed directly to the making of this book. Museum curators, archivists and librarians were invariably helpful and informative, while historians and other specialists were generous in supplying information and inspecting drafts. We're particularly grateful to:

Will Adams, David Anderson, Martin Angove, Gwenllian Ashley, Jeremy Atkinson, David Austin, Richard Bebb, Elisabeth Bennett, Edward Besly, Oliver Blackmore, Helen Bradley, Eva Bredsdorff, Sara Brown, Alun Burge, Barry Burnham, Noel Chanan, Claire Clancy, Kim Collis, Mary-Ann Constantine, Geoff Cook, Jane Davidson, Ceri Davies, Ken Davies, Ann Dorsett, Sara Downs, Susan Edwards, Garethe El-Tawab, Gavin Evans, Neil Evans, Stuart Evans, Janet Fletcher, Hywel Francis, Lynn Francis, Michael Freeman, Janet Fletcher, Phil Garratt, Hollie Gaze, Ralph Griffiths, Rhidian Griffiths, Helen Gwerfyl, Adam Gwilt, Helen Hallesy, Simon Hancock, Trevor Herbert, Stephanie Hines, Sue Hodges, Deian Hopkin, Alan Vaughan Hughes, Iestyn Hughes, Sioned Hughes, Richard Hughes, Richard Ireland, E. Wyn James, Heather James, Les James, Lowri Jenkins, Angela John, Aled Gruffydd Jones, Dinah Jones, Gareth Jones, Jen Jones, Meinir Pierce Jones, Robert Protheroe Jones, Janet Karn, Viv Kelly, Hilary and Paul Kennelly, John Koch, Katrina Legg, Maredudd ap Huw, Mark Lewis, Morwenna Lewis, Menna Morgan, Prys Morgan, David Morris, Karen Murdoch, Rhys Mwyn, Sue Newham, Eve Nicholson, D. Huw Owen, Elen Phillips, Benjamin Price, Phil Prosser, Siân Rees, Mark Redknap, Andrew Renton, Leigh Richardson, Sarah Roberts, Elfed Rowlands, Val Rowlands, Jane Rutherfoord, Rachel Silverson, Elen Wyn Simpson, Moyra Skenfield, Ian Smith, Mark Soady, Peter Stead, Richard Suggett, Hazel Thomas, Huw Thomas, M. Wynn Thomas, Ceri Thompson, Steve Thompson, Linda Tomos, Will Troughton, Geraint Tudur, Eben Upton, Richard Vroom, Peter Wakelin, Elizabeth Walker, Sue Walker, Chris West, Alison Weston, Deborah-Anne Wildgust, Eurwyn Wiliam, Emma Williams, Vivienne Williams, Siân Williams and Kate Woodward. Steve Burrow and Iwan ap Dafydd deserve special thanks for their invaluable help in coordinating work on objects in Amgueddfa Cymru – National Museum Wales and the National Library of Wales respectively.

The staff of Gwasg Gomer cared for the book at every stage, from its conception and early development to its appearance in the world. We're especially grateful to Meirion Davies, Cathryn Ings, Ceri Wyn Jones, Ashley Owen and Elinor Wyn Reynolds. Rebecca Ingleby Davies designed the book with ingenuity and care. Thanks to Rhodri Owen for correcting proofs.

Thanks are due to all the memory institutions who allowed their objects to be photographed and included in the book. Every effort has been made to contact copyright holders. We are grateful to the following for permission to reproduce items: Felinfoel Brewery (dragon logo), National Museums Scotland (Maesmor mace), A. M. Heath (A. J. Cronin, *The citadel*), Sarah Williams (David Jones, 'Cara Wallia derelicta'), Orion Publishing Group (R.S. Thomas, 'Llanrhaeadr ym Mochnant'), Wayne Thomas, NUM (Penrhiwceiber Lodge banner), Gwyneth Lewis ('Baptism at Llanbadarn'), Mary Lloyd Jones ('Ie / Yes'), Sain and Rolant Dafis ('For Tinkerbell') and Twm Morys ('Séance Watcyn Wynn'), Women's Archive Wales (factorywomensvoices.wales), National Library of Wales and Amgueddfa Cymru – National Museum Wales.

INDEX